MW00860657

LIFE IN FULL
Colors

LIFE IN FULL
Colors

UNLOCK YOUR CHILDLIKE CURIOSITY TO
UNCOVER AND ACTIVATE THE CREATIVE
INTELLIGENCE YOU ARE

Corry MacDonald

Copyright © 2020 by Corry MacDonald.

All rights reserved. No part of this publication may be reproduced, distributed, or transmitted in any form or by any means, including photocopying, recording, digital scanning, or other electronic or mechanical methods, without the prior written permission of the author, except in the case of brief quotations embodied in critical reviews and certain other noncommercial uses permitted by copyright law.

ISBN Paperback: 978-1-7354967-0-2
ISBN Electronic: 978-1-7354967-1-9

Library of Congress Control Number: 2020916283

Printed in the United States of America.

Corry MacDonald
corry@creativehealingwithcorry.com
www.CreatingHealingWithCorry.com

DISCLAIMER: The author of this book does not dispense medical advice or prescribe the use of any technique as a form of treatment for physical, emotional, or medical problems. The intent of the author is only to offer information of a general nature to help you in your quest for emotional and spiritual well-being. In the event you use any of the information in this book, the author and the publisher assume no responsibility for your actions. Thank you.

Welcome Note from
Corry

When I began to write this book several years ago, it was from a place that felt forced, like I was not truly ready. It was clear to me I had some living and growing to do. I had several challenges to own and subsequently leverage for my learning, upcycling, and transformation. This is the process I am going to teach you in this book—how to take any personal challenge you experience and shift it to create something beautiful.

I know now that if what I create flows in from a Higher Place with a power far beyond me, then it is meant to be shared out into the world. This book flowed into written form steadily and with a speed that surprised me during the first lockdown of

COVID-19 while I was living in Dubai. Tucked into a quiet room at home, I would begin each day in the silence of my heart and received the words in these pages as Divine downloads.

One thing you will notice is when I refer to our Higher Power, I use various names interchangeably. Names such as Divine, Creator, Source, and Creative Intelligence. As I wrote, I welcomed all the words I received and recorded them as they came. They point to the same timeless, formless, Universal life energy that we all share, as it is ultimately pure love. Substitute the name(s) that resonate most for you as you read.

I am more than grateful for all the family, friends, clients, and unseen Divine Guides who helped to bring this book into form simply by being part of my journey to discovering how to live my Life in Full Colors. I dedicate this book to you all with a special dedication to my beautiful, colorful family. I love you.

Because I have lived almost half of my life overseas, an amazing adventure that both my husband and I chose for our family, complete with its own set of challenges, I have a big place in my heart for displaced people. When I consider immigrants and refugees who lack the luxury of choice, who must leave their country due to trauma, only to arrive in a new culture to experience more pain, such as anti-immigrant sentiment, I am moved to give my support.

This is why I am donating all net proceeds from the sales of this book, *Life in Full Colors,* to the Vancouver Island Counselling Centre for Immigrants and Refugees (VICCIR). VICCIR is a non-profit, charitable group that provides various forms of support, including art therapy, "for those immigrants and refugees suffering the impact of trauma." I resonate with their vision, which implores "all citizens to contribute to communities that thrive on diversity of origin, culture, religion and interests, and are strengthened by shared common values."

As VICCIR is based in the province of British Columbia, which is where I completed my art therapy training, I am grateful to align with such a big-hearted team who share my Canadian roots. Roots which gave me the wings to fly far so that I could grow, learn, and share this way.

To learn more about VICCIR or how you can donate visit www.viccir.org.

Contents

LIFE IN FULL
Colors

"With everything that has happened to you, you can either feel sorry for yourself or treat what has happened as a gift. Everything is either an opportunity to grow or an obstacle to keep you from growing. You get to choose."

—Wayne Dyer

Tools for Your Journey

Please note: Before you begin reading this book, it's important that you know that there are several creative exercises throughout the upcoming chapters for you to embody the learning. To participate and receive the fullest experience for yourself, you will need these basic art materials, most of which can be found within your home. For our work here, it's best to use children's art supplies rather than fine art supplies. This way you can relax, play with the colors, and enjoy the process without worrying about the product.

Here are the simple art materials you will need:

1. White paper (simple bond) or a sketchbook (11 x 17" or A3 size) to provide lots of creative space.
2. Colored crayons or pastels in basic sets of either 8 or 12. Some people like oil pastels

while others prefer chalk. I recommend both if possible.

3. Colored markers, also in a set of 8 or 12.
4. Children's tempera paint "cake set" of 8 or 12 colors (the kind with the hard round disks of paint that only require you to dip a wet brush in to use directly). These are paints are most commonly found in a small rectangular case with a lid that snaps shut on top.
5. Paint brushes of a few different sizes. I recommend buying a set of three or five in sizes and shapes that make you curious to use them.
6. Journal or notebook and a pen you enjoy writing with.
7. Glue stick.
8. Pair of scissors.

We Begin Within

"The infinite wonders of the universe are revealed to us in exact measure as we are capable of receiving them. The keenness of our vision depends not on how much we can see, but on how much we feel."

—Helen Keller

Chapter 1

Shake Things Up: How Depression, Direct Advice, and Disaster Woke Me Up

Imagine yourself as a child lying back in a bed of pine needles under evergreen branches. With eyes full of wonder, see yourself catching countless white clumps of heavy snow falling from an inky-blue sky. This is how I remember enjoying many winter evenings as a little girl growing up in Canada. I felt most at home within the quiet hug of the natural world outside.

Hold that picture in one hand while you take hold of another picture in complete contrast to the first. Here again, we see a child—me again. This time I am tucked into the quiet playhouse within my kindergarten classroom, surrounded by rambunctious children playing freely throughout the space where I stand—nervous, fearful, and alone, peeking out from behind the window.

These two pictures, while contrasting in so many ways, are also descriptive of our human story in general. While there is a curious and wonder-filled part of us connected to the Universe, a closed-off, cautious self who prefers to sit safely on the sidelines exists as well.

Fear Takes the Front Seat

Over time, in my little story, this more fearful version of Corry began to show up more often than the free and fearless one. From a very early age, I had been conditioned to expect things to feel unsafe and unpredictable. I grew up in a home where the tools needed for healthy family communication and stability were lacking. Even when I tried to lighten up, there was a voice in my head that kept me stuck.

For much of my teenage life, and into my thirties, I listened to that relentless voice in my overthinking and ruminating mind. This created a strong downward pull into sadness and mistrust in myself and others. I would try to outrun it by diving into friendships, jobs, and commitments, thinking, *This time it will be different*, but the entrenched pathway of my programmed thinking mind was far more powerful than any of the desires of my heart.

With my mind judging everything as a danger or a threat all the time, as soon as I would start something with the hope of bringing something meaningful and lasting into my life, I would suddenly pull away, quit, or disappear behind the window of a false, forced smile of protection where I felt most "at home."

My perfected happy face masked my fears and came everywhere with me. It joined along when my husband James and I jumped at an opportunity to move across the globe for work in Yokohama, Japan. This would be the first of several stops in our international journey. I was excited to go and put distance between myself and the unhealthy family and cultural dynamics that I felt were pulling me down at that point in time.

While distance helped in a way, what surfaced, however, was a deep sense of isolation. Especially as time went on and I became a young mother of three. Disconnected from both my family and my Higher Power, another part of my life that I had let go of along the way, I lost connection with my childlike Universal Self.

This rift sent me spiraling down into a heavy inner sadness that overtook me and often confused those around me; it just wouldn't fully lift. Over time, I came to understand that this inner sadness had deep roots. During my childhood, my parents were in a lot of pain, which stemmed from their own families' dysfunction from when they were small children. With no tools at the time to heal their personal traumas, they simply passed them on to me and my sisters unknowingly.

As a little child, I could sense the stress and strain of their suppressed fear and anger humming below the surface of our family's day-to-day. Sporadically and unpredictably, it would erupt in ways that scared, surprised, and confused me.

I have now come to understand that this fear-based anger—a pattern I have repeated in my own life—is what co-dependents feel when they give their power away in hopes that another will save them from their pain. The anger and resentment we feel appears to be directed at those around us but is actually aimed at ourselves for being so needy and feeling stuck in victimhood.

My mom's ever-present stress and resentment at having to be the main caregiver to four little girls coupled with my dad's drinking, his absences due to travel with his work, and then his unpredictable mood swings when he was at home with us were absorbed by me at a very early age. Known as "the sensitive one" in my family for my emotional outbursts, I developed a core belief that life was unsafe and that as a sensitive person, I couldn't navigate things as well as the others.

By the time I was in grade school, my mom sought some sort of order and structure for our family. That led us to church, as was typical within the culture I came from. While some beautiful aspects ultimately came into my life through those church days—such as coming to know the difference between fear-based religion and heart-based spirituality—as a child growing up within an oftentimes confusing and contradictory belief system, it only deepened the conditioning I had already begun to receive at home. This being to hide and contain my heavy, painful emotions while creating a bright and shiny surface in order to appear highly competent, positive, and happy.

I was not alone in this either. I laugh now at the memory of my three sisters and our parents driving to church, all in full fight-mode, yelling in the van the whole way, only to hop out fully reconfigured with bright smiles and "God bless you's" for everyone outside. What made it worse was I really thought that this was the way all people *should* behave, as I observed it all around me both in the church culture and within society, even though it wasn't authentic and felt dishonest to me.

Still, it was all I knew and it continued to be my *go-to* way of handling my heaviness through my 20s and into my early 30s. While it seems like a dream to write all of this now, knowing how much has changed since those early days, back when I was a young mother of three, it was my main mode of operating. I knew I was in need of a miracle, yet at that point in time, I highly doubted there could be one for me.

My Miracle Moment

And then it happened; in a moment, everything shook me up. Literally. It was 2011, and I was on a tightly packed train traveling back from Tokyo, on my way home from a first-time session with a new therapist, a warm, deeply intuitive woman who had just given me the support and the direct guidance that my heart had long been crying out for. By this point, I had been suffering from depression for some time, so to leave her feeling curious, even a little hopeful, was a big thing in itself.

She had really shaken me up, in a good way. She said the depression I'd been stuck in for the past several years was due to a rift between who I thought I should be for others and my Authentic

Self. Appealing to the artist within me, she told me to start over, to turn everything upside down, and begin each day by sitting in absolute silence with my paints—no more retelling my victim story and no more running around saying "Yes" to everyone— joining endless coffee mornings and helping each person and committee who asked for my support, only to return home to my children and husband depleted and resentful that I said "Yes" again. Nothing more. Nothing less. I held her words like a lifeline.

She promised that if I was faithful to myself in this way, if I was watchful, things would change for me and, in turn, they would change for all the people around me. She used the analogy of a mobile hanging from the ceiling, where when one piece is touched, all the pieces move. She warned me that some people on the mobile would not want me to change—some people would prefer the over-giving, pasted-on-smile version of me to stay put—but to not let that deter me.

As I wrote everything down in my journal on the train ride home, I wondered what it might look like if I really took her advice. Suddenly, the train jarred and lurched forward, wildly—the infamous earth-quake that triggered a devastating tsunami had hit Japan and left all of us passengers trapped under-ground for several hours.

So much transpired during those hours that I could write a whole book about it, but for now I want to focus on two key discoveries that changed my life miraculously. I would never have guessed that those hours spent underground would become a doorway to Awakening to Life.

More Love Than Words Can Convey

The first key discovery was how much love and Universal Intelligence is flowing to us through an ever-present silence, which our noisy lives drown out completely. My therapist had mentioned the importance of connecting to this Divine Silence, and I actually experienced this intimately that life-changing day.

See, when you sit in a train full of people in this sort of situation, one you have never before found yourself in, so much happens in your head. You wonder, *What's going on?* with no idea how it will play out. *How bad is it? Is this the big one that was supposed to hit Japan? What's happening out there?* I had so many questions and nobody to ask. Nobody had any answers amid all the confusion that day.

Instead, I found myself listening to the Divine Silence, which was so strong in contrast to the continual aftershocks. I could hear my innermost self so clearly as I turned within. The silence on that dark train was oddly beautiful. It took me somewhere that felt strangely familiar, perhaps how I felt as a child snuggled up in the falling snow. Words cannot really capture it, but if I could choose a few words, they would be the following:

- deep calm
- slow stillness
- beyond fear ·
- pure knowing
- circling warmth
- pulsing life

The sublime silence I felt so deeply in the midst of all that upheaval was a profound contrast to the confusion and discord all around me, in my life as well as on that train. I was shocked to become aware of this new wave of calm spreading through me as waves of aftershocks shook the train. I was a stranger among strangers, trapped underground. But I felt deep inner peace.

My Commitment to My Self

That's when I experienced another key learning, then and there, sitting on the floor, wrapped up in that still point inside. From a place deep within, I suddenly made a commitment to my Higher Power that when I got out of that train, I would be true to my therapist's words. I would shift everything up. I would begin my days in colors and silence. I would choose my life and rediscover what I loved. It was crystal clear that the silence within me was uncovering all these hidden impulses—another beautiful key.

And then, suddenly, it all shifted, the moment we got a "clear track" signal. The train inched forward toward the light until, ever so slowly, it limped its way up to the station and we all made our way up to the surface to stumble out into the sunlight. Each of us figuring our way back to our families and homes.

As I ran toward my husband and children, I replayed the commitment I had made to the Universe. My promise to shift my life's mobile around played over and over in my mind each time the soles of my running feet hit the ground. No longer was this Higher Love "out there," disconnected and uncaring. I could feel it closer than close, pulsing deep within me as I did when I was a little girl, wonder-filled and free. Little did I know then that all the learning my soul needed to make that shift was embedded in my train tunnel earthquake experience.

A New Way Opens Up

Soon after the earthquake, I stuck to the commitment I made to the Universe as a way suddenly opened up to help others. Two dear friends had been to a high school shelter up north in Ishinomaki, a city hit hard by the tsunami. They were heading back up and asked me to join them. They knew that using art as a therapeutic support was important to me and they felt it could be of great benefit for those in the shelters too.

This would be my first experience in assisting others to create healing for themselves. With no formal training and no real plan other than to provide an outlet for people to tell their stories expressively, I gathered art supplies from friends and neighbors who were more than willing to donate and help out. The earth was still rumbling, and the world was watching the Fukushima nuclear power plant nervously. We hauled everything up to the shelter and laid crayons, clay, and paper out on a blue plastic tarp for people to sit, create, and take as they needed.

People gathered. They drew pictures. They pressed and formed clay with their hands, often making black snakes, a symbol many used to represent the tsunami that churned up the volcanic black sand. They folded origami paper into neat, crisp shapes and shared painful stories: lost loved ones, lost homes, the loss of the lives they had known before the tsunami came. I was deeply moved by their stories and touched by how, in spite of all their challenges, they continued to find ways to help others struggling, even in the midst of their pain.

My few days in that school gymnasium were filled with more learning than I could ever have imagined. Being with the people who sat on that blue tarp, sharing their stories with me as they set out to rebuild their lives amid disaster, changed me.

I experienced the Creative Intelligence and authenticity radiating from all the beautiful people calmly responding to their extraordinary challenges in ways that humbled and inspired me. Moment by moment, surrounded by hope and quiet strength, I started to believe in a new way forward for me.

More Learning Comes In

Trusting a strong impulse to apply for formal art therapy training, I got accepted and completed my training via distance learning with the Vancouver Art Therapy Institute. Simultaneously, I enrolled in an Integral Art Therapy course offered by expressive art therapist Eri Yoshida on a strong impulse toward my personal healing. Over time, Eri became a mentor and a dear friend.

I learned how to deepen my connection with the Universal Intelligence within me, how to feel my emotions and express them with all my unique colors to receive the Divine guidance flowing to me. I came to know and love my colorful self, every shade and hue. This love naturally poured outward to the people and situations in each area of my life. Day by day, I began to live Life in Full Colors.

After completing my art therapy training, my family and I moved to Bangkok. I opened an art studio to help others discover and experience their innate Creative Intelligence so that they too could live and love every color and piece within. As I worked with more and more people, all from different cultures, classes, ages, and genders, I recognized that the discoveries we were making took a similar shape. Over time, I understood: our fear-filled, heavy-hued challenges show up in our lives time and again until we turn toward them for the teaching they hold for us.

This is what I learned from my own miracle moment that woke me up and from the miracle moments of those I have worked with—while none of us share the same miracle moment, we do share the same heart at the center of them. Big, little, dark, light—all moments are one and the same.

We need to own such moments. Sit with the fear. Be with the struggle. Welcome the pain and uncover what is tucked beneath it. Trust the process. Expect a miracle. Find the gift.

Facing Fear to Find a New Focus

I saw this happen for Talia, a soft-spoken woman who joined one of my workshops to discover that she took up very little space in her own life. While she had a sense that her vibrancy had been swallowed by her new role as a practical-minded at-home mother, it wasn't until she saw it reflecting back at her from her artwork that she realized how small her self-worth had become.

Amid a chatty group busily creating magazine collages to express who they perceived themselves to be, Talia sat pensively. The emptiness of her large white paper engulfed the only image she managed to set into her collage—a lone peering eye. For Talia I could see this eye felt almost unbearable to own. And yet, that is exactly what she did. As she looked into the eye surrounded by all that white space, it looked straight back at her. At first, she gazed back disturbingly, as the expanse of emptiness echoed back the emptiness she felt inside.

Then, as she grew easier with it, that lone eye, initially piercing and judgmental, transformed for Talia. Now she had a focused partner to help her to look below the surface. Her artwork became an invitation to honor the silent space within her life, as in the collage, allowing Talia to be intentional with what she chose to fill that space. As she listened inwardly to the Creative Intelligence within her, she recognized she could now consider her happiness and explore her life as a blank page waiting to be filled.

What followed that powerful pivot point were many more moments for Talia using art to express her innermost self. To her delight, her color-filled creations became more and more vibrant and radiant, as did her life. Recognizing she had uncovered her passion, she took up a series of art lessons until one day she began to introduce herself as an artist. Talia uncovered a whole dimension of herself by literally moving through the eye of her personal storm to allow the fullest expression of herself out.

What Unopened Gifts Sit Within You?

I wonder what unseen potentials are tucked inside you? You might be wondering if you are poised to live a Life in Full Colors right now; to bring Creative Healing into and through every challenge in your life. After working with hundreds of people, I know your potentials are limitless and are waiting for you to dovetail with your Creative Intelligence to uncover them.

Perhaps you can feel that pulsing Love Force within you right now, filled with impulses unique to your precious life journey. You are now receiving the unique invitation to step into a whole new experience of yourself as a Creative Healer. A space where you can choose to show up in each moment in a whole new rhythm rather than defaulting to reactivity each time people, things, and events in your outer world don't resonate with your idea of what *should be*. You are invited—as I was many years ago—to "shake things up" completely!

This book is an open door to enter into a totally new understanding of what's playing out before you. It's your time now to learn how to activate the innate Creative Intelligence within you so that you can walk right up to any challenge in your life fearlessly and have the tools in hand to pivot its heavy hues and transform the situation for lightness.

So, my dear Creative One, are you ready to take this next step? Are you ready to walk straight through and into a journey of Creating a Life in Full Colors for yourself? If your whole body, mind, and spirit are saying "YES!", then you are well on your way. Just turn the page (like a key in a door) and let's begin.

Chapter 2

Wake Things Up: Time to Shift Your Focus Inwardly

W ell done! You've turned that page like you've opened a door, and now you're in! A space and place you've never been before. Breathe in and feel the freshness of the moment. It's all here for you! Know that you are very welcome here. Make yourself at home; I've been waiting for you.

Now that you're at this starting point of your Life in Full Colors journey, it's time for you turn your focus inwardly. Here you will shift into the *just right* mental space so that you can easily enter all the places that this book will allow you to explore.

Inhale deeply, right down to the tips of your toes; sit up tall and shake any sleepiness from your system because this chapter is here to wake up any part of you that might still be dozing off and unaware of the creative power tucked inside of you.

Wake Up to Where We Are Going Wrong

What does it actually mean to wake up? We hear the word "awakening" a lot now, yet it can be easily misunderstood. Some get confused and think it's about being in a state of pure positivity every hour of every day. In actuality this only creates more stress in the end. So, let's slow down here to take a closer look and see where we can avoid steering off course.

Let's start with "awakening," shall we? Awakening is that miracle-filled moment within your human experience when you uncover and realize yourself as pure watchful Awareness with a capital A—the process of untangling from the self-concept that you are the *doer* of your life while unhooking from the messy, knotted string of overthinking amid all that doing.

If you're still here reading, then you have most likely experienced a still point within you where you became conscious of yourself as the one observing all that is playing out before you. You recognize that you are not the one tangled up in the scenes called "my life" as you once thought yourself to be. While awakening brings great freedom with this shift in perception, either coming suddenly or in spurts and stages, it can be emotionally painful because many of your identities, conditioning, and beliefs once held so tightly lose their grip and fade away.

Awakening—What It's Not

Awakening is not the same thing as the "just keep it light and positive" mindset that many self-helpers ascribe to. This is not about avoiding heavy emotions to keep it light. And yet, a natural by-product of waking up is a deep joy that radiates silently from within. Genuine joy flows out effortlessly as you unplug from your fear-based conditioning.

This is not the same as glossing over heaviness with a thinly painted-on smile as if to say "everything's fine" when it's not. Trying to be positive all the time is simply not sustainable nor is it honest. Most of all, it will only bring trouble when those heavier emotions get piled up so high that they start to overflow.

It's always beautiful to see this positivity facade crumble when I invite people to play their colors and shapes onto paper to express whatever heavy emotions they are experiencing. I remember one woman in particular, with her gentle and quiet way, sharing in surprise with the group, "All my life I was told to just focus on the sunny side of life. It's been my way of living for so long I didn't even know I cut myself off from feeling all of my feelings!"

I've heard others say they "didn't want to bring the group down" with their sad feelings and emotions. And yet, when we choose to feel, express, and share all the colors of our whole selves, we open the door of opportunity for others to see our true colors. This is being awakened to all we are, which invites those around us to feel connected to all that shines out through our vulnerability.

When Outward Focusing Takes Over

The truth is that many people have no idea how much brilliant radiance is tucked inside of them. Sadly, most people are living life focused outwardly so as to avoid feeling the trapped emotions within them by *overdoing* their outer life. As introspection gets buried by busyness, the inner disconnection only widens.

For some, this means getting crazily stressed out, *over-busying* and filling up a schedule to beyond full so as not to dare stop and feel what's going on inside. For others, this can look like *over-giving* to everything and everyone else in order to feel enough. Of course, this only causes resentment and burnout. While for others still, it means numbing out by *binging*—in any number of ways, including food, alcohol, social media, shopping, even exercising—to disconnect and avoid hidden feelings within.

Whether you tend toward one of these overdoing modes or a combination doesn't matter. What does matter is that you wake up to the fact that you are a highly creative *being*, not a *doing*, and learn how to enjoy the experience of doing from a place of inspiration rather than from compulsion.

We Need to Look at Our Minds in a Whole New Way

To step forward into being, it's essential to turn your gaze from looking outwardly to inwardly. Get your keychain ready because it's time for you to receive a special key for your journey. I call this key "Begin Within," as it enables you to look at everything from the inside out and move through your moments in a whole new way.

This is especially important when things on the outside are not looking so good.

Now, you're likely scratching your head and wondering what in the world I'm talking about. Choosing to Begin Within can be challenging initially, especially when you have so many things vying for your attention. To help you make this inward turn, let's take a fresh look at your mind.

Did you know that within you are two very different minds? The clearest explanation of this came to me from Dr. Anne Jensen as I learned her emotional healing and stress-reduction technique, HeartSpeak.

Most of us are very familiar with our Thinking Mind, which is the linear, rational, and explaining mind. The Thinking Mind is an incredible problem-solving machine that can keep us safe and help us survive. It can even locate problems to solve when there aren't any! Like a monster sprouting seven heads, which, in turn, will each sprout seven more, it will go on and on if not kept in check.

Less explored and often not integrated is our Feeling Mind, which is unpredictable, heart-based, imaginal, and a seeker of inner truth. Because it is so opposite to our logical Thinking Mind, it often is disregarded and seen as too chaotic and unreliable to give any serious attention to. However, in both my personal and professional experience, this inner disconnection from the Feeling Mind is at the core of whatever needs healing.

Science gives us important data on the Feeling Mind. We know from research done by the Heart-Math Institute that our heart sends far more signals to the brain than the brain sends to the heart. In fact, our heart's electromagnetic field is 5000 times stronger than the brain's magnetic field! Clearly, our feeling hearts matter.

Our Big Box of Emotions

And yet, even with all of the research revealing the power of our feeling hearts, what can keep us stuck in overdoing is that a greater part of us knows there's a big ol' sealed-up box of emotions buried inside. Emotions that haven't been touched for many years. The thought of going toward those emotions is far from enticing because of the way we have been taught to label them.

Growing up, most of us pick up a belief that light emotions, such as happiness and joy, are good and can be embraced, while heavy emotions, such as fear and disgust, are bad and should be hidden away. Rarely are we taught that our emotions are filled with Divine Intelligence and that it is far more helpful to perceive them as light and heavy rather than good and bad. With this conditioning, it's understandable to see people running around, stressed out and super busy, doing all they can to numb out and avoid any heaviness within.

What I am inviting you to step into now is something new that most of us weren't taught to do. I'm opening a way for you to deepen your awareness around all of your emotions in this journey ahead.

Perhaps the easiest way to explain it is by asking you to imagine a big box of crayons filled with emotions. Go ahead and lift the lid and scan the full range of hues. Notice how some are light and others are heavy? Yet all are an essential part of the box and necessary to complete the set. If you think of emotions this way, then you can form a new perspective and become inspired to dive within and relate to your varied emotions anew.

Like a child holding a big 120-count box of crayons, you can unleash your curiosity and wonder for what's to come of all these colors. Only when you can step into the ease of this upshifted perspective will you feel free to explore and embrace all the radiance that is hidden within you.

Workshop Wisdom

When I invite workshop participants to express their emotions creatively, some rely on their habit of overdoing to help them out. Imagine a buffet of paper, paints in a rainbow of colors, and a full array of chalk and oil pastels. For those in their creative flow, this display is enticing, while for a new participant, it can be intimidating. Oftentimes, a first timer will gather far more art materials from the available selection than they end up using.

I find this to be such a wonderful example of our human tendency toward overdoing when trying something new. We tend to ignore our Feeling Mind to intuit what we actually need. There's no doubt that it is a big step to drop out of the Thinking Mind in order to play our emotions out with art materials this way for the first time.

Of course, it's only natural that, when given a task that's new and unfamiliar, one would listen to their active Thinking Mind commanding them to "Take as many supplies as you can carry! You need to be fully prepared!" because logically, more materials will help solve any problems that may arise. Yet when everyone settles into their creative space and gets in their natural flow, they can relax and sense into the exact art materials their Creative Intelligence wants them to use.

That pile of leftover art materials that ends up not being needed is much like the protective layer from the Thinking Mind. Once the Feeling Mind has some space to be expressed, both minds can integrate and work together congruently to bring the relevant information and emotions onto the paper as Creative Intelligence in clear view.

The Road Ahead for You

As you continue on with your Begin Within key, simply stop, breathe, and take a moment to consider the inner access that this key gives you. As you hold it in your hand, enjoy anticipating what your heart-felt, colorful range of emotions can unlock in you.

It's a transformational journey ahead for you. There are seven steps to learn (and to embody in a playful way) up ahead. Each step is here to support you and teach you how to create the Life in Full Colors you came to this world to experience.

Like an upcycling artist who uses discarded and broken materials to create a masterpiece, you too will learn to do the same thing with your life. By picking out any one of your current life challenges as your ultimate art material, you will learn these seven steps for Creating a Life in Full Colors from it—how to Own It, Ask on It, Receive from It, Act on It, Expect It, Love It, and Share It—so that you can shape it into something valuable and completely new.

It's Time to Go...

Knowing all that is waiting for you around the bend of the next page, you're likely wide awake now and curious to get going. That's exactly the state to be in for your journey ahead. Approach every opportunity in the coming pages like that expectant child holding a big box of crayons and watch what happens. You will not be disappointed!

So now, take your keychain and slide your new Begin Within key into the ignition because it's time to go!

Ready, set, start it up!

Feel the hum of the motor as you open your window to catch the breeze.

You are more than ready to begin your adventure with all that you now know. And remember, enjoy the ride; it's going to be a wonder-filled one!

Refresh and Review

- Awakening is a big-moment perception shift that brings great freedom, either suddenly or, more often, in stages. It also can be challenging, as it reveals the identities and conditioning within you that are unhelpful and no longer needed.

- Favoring positivity while ignoring heavier feelings and emotions is not being true to yourself.

- Many people are *overdoing* life (either by *over-busying, binging, or over-giving*) so that they don't have to feel the array of heavy emotions within them.

- It's important to recognize that all emotions are filled with Divine Intelligence, and it is helpful to refer to them as heavy and light (rather than bad and good).

- Knowing the Feeling Mind is our heart's creative center while the Thinking Mind is the problem-flagging center motivates us to use both in powerful alignment.

Creative Spark

Feeling Mind and Thinking Mind

- Take a piece of paper and fold it in half. On one side at the top of the page draw a heart shape and on the other side draw the outline of a brain.

- Open a box of colored markers and choose a color that feels good. Below the heart, begin to write all the ways that you live from your Feeling Mind. Perhaps you follow your gut feeling and instincts very well. If so, write that down. Are you the impulsive one in the family who will suggest a sudden weekend away? Do you find it easy to laugh and cry at the movies? Just note all the unique ways your Feeling Mind is experienced by you without judgment or analysis.

- Repeat this process for your Thinking Mind underneath your brain drawing. Close your eyes and consider all the ways you express your Thinking Mind each day. Perhaps you are extremely good at organization in your work or in your family's finances. You may be the one who never forgets anyone's birthday. Do your family and friends refer to you as the "Rational One"? Whatever comes through for you, jot it all down without judgment.

- Once you're done, simply look at the page with open curiosity. Notice which side of the page filled easily and which side was more challenging. Sense if you operate more from your Thinking Mind or from your Feeling Mind. Perhaps you will discover you have a good balance of the two and have integrated them both. Or maybe you tend toward one more than the other. Regardless, don't judge yourself; use your inner observer to see where you are at with these two minds here and now at the start of your journey.

- Set an intention for yourself to integrate these two minds of yours during your journey ahead. Write that intention down clearly like this: "I intend to integrate my Thinking and Feeling Minds now!"

- Loop it with bright colors or underline it in a bold blast of hues to celebrate the start of your journey! Your words hold great power, which you can amplify by feeling deeply into your heart as you read your intention aloud, inviting all the forces in the Universe to join you!

**Imagine this taking place for you now—
See it, feel it, be it!**

Chapter 3

Set Things Up:
Time to Prepare Your
Creative Space

All right, Creative One, you're on the road now; your journey has begun. For you to be successful it's essential to understand the necessity of preparing your inner and outer space. Let's slow down a little because what you're about to learn is foundational.

Do I detect a bit of curiosity in you right now? I sure hope so. It's a beautiful way to be—lit up with wonderment! There's so much goodness up ahead for you. Let's get started.

We'll first discuss your inner space and how important it is to bring it into stillness in order to create. If you're one of the many naysayers who's taking this in and saying, "But I'm *really not* creative; I can't even draw a stickman!", then this chapter will be especially important for you.

Contrary to what you think, whether you are conscious of it or not, you are creating all the time at the level of thought. We'll take a closer look at this too. Remember what the Creative Spark in the last chapter taught you about the power in the words you use? Now is a great time to choose a new way to speak of your creative self. You might try, "I'm uncovering and activating my unlimited Creative Intelligence."

Finally, you will learn how to set up your own unique creative space in your home. A special place to support you as you create. I'll give you some helpful tips so that you can design a warm, inviting space to relax in—a place you feel drawn to (no pun intended!).

What's the Big Deal about Space?

Have you ever looked forward to staying overnight someplace new, maybe a cozy little inn or a new boutique hotel, only to find yourself disappointed because the vibe of the space kept you from relaxing into it?

There can be many reasons for this, of course. Maybe it was so full of clutter it left you no room to breathe. Maybe the noise outside on the street kept you up all night. Maybe the room was so sparse that it felt soulless and sad. Regardless of the reason, you didn't feel at ease being there.

The importance of creating the right space became very clear to me in my first art therapy practicum set in an international preschool. The school was beautiful and filled with sensorially rich areas to stimulate the children's aesthetic senses. Colorful interactive displays dotted the perimeter to attract and engage the students along with several open spaces to encourage wider exploration.

I remember my supervisor instructing me to create a blank white space within the preschool to hold children's art therapy sessions in. Dutifully, I hung some long white curtains to form a tiny rectangular space. The makeshift room stood apart, nestled by a wide window, in the corner of the art room. All that this cozy space could hold was a wee children's table, four small stools, and some art supplies tucked into an inbuilt shelf.

It wasn't long after I created the corner art therapy space that curious children began poking their small, sweet faces between the curtain openings and smiling their approval. Before I knew it, somehow that white hug of a room got named "the cloud." I can't remember who named it that, whether it came from the giggling children or the watchful adults, but "the cloud" became a sought-out place to be. Amid all the bustling outside its white walls, "the cloud" provided a calm and soothing retreat, not only for the children in my practicum sessions but also for the entire preschool community—teachers, students, and cleaning staff too!

Each one of us needs spaces of solitude in our loud and busy world. While "the cloud" was a seemingly simple physical space made from a few white curtains defining a boundary within a preschool, it taught me so many things. The main thing being how necessary it is to have an access point in the outer world to open us wide to our inner world, which is the home of our Creative Intelligence; the very essence of who we all are! It's from this silent vastness that we can feel and imagine something new.

Space for the New to Come Through

When there's no space to stop, be still, and listen within, how can anything new feel welcome to show up for a little visit with you? A clear and quiet space supports you even when you don't realize you need the respite it provides. Like an instant thought-de-cluttering machine, it can ease you right into your Feeling Mind so that you can become aware of what your intuition is telling you.

Contrary to the loud flurry of activity and busyness that we can get ourselves swept up in, we human beings all share a strong pull to the quiet. It's said that half of us are introverts, and even those who label themselves as extroverts have a streak of intro-version in them. We all need to tuck into the still space within us to recharge from time to time.

We're quite like our cellphones; after going full out for a while, eventually the battery goes flat. So, with the same intensity you monitor your phone battery and tend to those downward-moving bars, I invite you to tend to your inner quiet with even more care.

For some of you, that may look like rising earlier to sit in the morning silence, while for others, it may mean some moments of peaceful reflection before bed. Perhaps a few pockets of stillness throughout the course of your day is best for you to access the Infinite Wisdom within you. Whichever of these opportunities for inner stillness resonates to bring "the cloud" experience into the rhythm of your day, trust and follow through.

Nothing lasting will shift within you unless you do something new and form gaps of gorgeous quiet in your day, structured specially for you! To begin, I suggest that you notice when your energy is at its best and then schedule yourself in for your inner quiet time. Prioritizing your self-care this way will be of great benefit to you and everyone. This will become very clear through our time together.

Become intentional about this and recognize that you are the one creating your life with each choice you make. You can choose to nourish yourself. Much like a plant that naturally reaches for the sun, you too can move toward what uplifts and benefits you.

If you're still unsure and would like some help accessing the spaciousness within you, try my free guided meditation at www.creatinghealingwith-corry.com. It's there for you to experience the love and joy within you. I assure you, once you connect inwardly with this most spacious part of yourself, you will visit regularly.

"But I'm Not an Artist!"

Now, if you are one of the many naysayers still believing your "I'm not creative!" thoughts, then I'm going to take this moment to share the truth with you. It's essential that you recognize who you are now so you can move through this book with no doubt that you are indeed a creative powerhouse and the artist of your life, regardless of what stories you've got going inside your head.

Let's stop and talk about creativity from the perspective of art therapy as you get set to prepare your outer creative space. Keeping it easy here, let's pause for a moment and take a good look at those two words—"art" and "therapy"—one at a time so it's very clear.

Just look at the word "art," and as you do, simply notice any ideas or images that show up in your mind's eye, perhaps of famous artists and galleries; then, let them pass on by. Why? Because they won't serve you on this journey. They have their place, but they are not useful for our purposes.

Try thinking of "art" as colorful energy flowing directly from your Feeling Mind. Imagine a preschooler racing out of the classroom with a massive grin while holding a dripping wet, spontaneous painting of pure energy in motion. *This* is the kind of "art" you are invited to make here with me. So, relax, exhale any stress you're feeling, and get ready to enjoy yourself.

Now, it's time to stop and look at that second word, "therapy." Its Latin root, *therapia,* means "to attend to." In your upcoming journey of Creating a Life in Full Colors, you will be attending to your growth and transformation. I can't think of anything better to attend to! Can you?

From the space of this book into the space of your life, you can see that creating a Life in Full Colors has nothing to do with making a beautiful painting to hang on the wall. Rather, it has got everything to do with attending to your most creative center—your beautiful feeling heart. That part of you filled with emotions longing to be expressed to reveal what you want for your life so that you can attract it to you.

Watch the Law of Attraction Make It Grow

The Universal Law of Attraction spells this out for us very clearly. Whatever we are focusing our thoughts and emotions on expands in our experience. Like a magnet, we attract more of the same. This can be fantastic when we're inwardly aligned and awake to our thoughts, feelings, and emotions. However, when we're not connected with our inner world, it can be debilitating. Universal Intelligence does not discriminate; until we change our focus and upshift our vibration, our attraction point stays the same.

This law works universally, leaving it up to each creative being to stop, feel in, and choose what thoughts and feelings they want to attract more of. Can you sense how essential it is to give yourself gaps of spacious silence so that you unplug from the outer noise, listen in, and bring both your Feeling and Thinking Minds into alignment?

As you give it more attention and space in your life, the Feeling Mind being (connected directly to your heart center) will naturally align with your Thinking Mind to attract what you want to create for your life. As you choose to focus upon something you want (Thinking Mind) and then feel it is already a part of your experience (Feeling Mind), you create a new vibration, shaping your reality anew through the Law of Attraction.

Sounds easy, right? For those who mostly operate in their Thinking Minds, this can seem impossible to do. I assure you it's not impossible. Simply allow yourself the space, from the quiet, observing part of you, to pay attention to how you're feeling more often. This will help to integrate your two minds.

It's within you to choose thoughts and actions that feel wonderful to you, and with practice it becomes easier to do. Be gentle with yourself and retain that curiosity that propelled you into this book.

Time to Create Your Own "Cloud"

Let's now apply what you've learned about your inner space outwardly. Ready to design your outer creative space to hold and support you through this journey and beyond?

Take a moment to consider all the beautiful places in nature you enjoy visiting, like a lush green forest or a vast empty beach. Notice the absence of devices, clocks, crowds, and jarring noise there. Go ahead—close your eyes and imagine your favorite spots to retreat to. Take your time. I'll be here when you return.

Keeping the feelings alive that this imagined visit sparked in you, pick up your favorite colored pen and, without thinking, simply flow a steady stream of words that capture what you saw, felt, and experienced into the space provided for you. Don't edit or analyze what you write; simply stay in your Feeling Heart and let your Creative Intelligence flow!

Let your eyes float over all the words you wrote down and notice which ones seem to jump out at you. Circle those words because they are filled with information for you. There's a certain sense about your outer creative space that your Higher Power is bringing to your attention. Write down your circled words and notice if an overall theme emerges (such as "sunny cove" or "silent haven"); jot those words down too. This is all helpful information coming from your Creative Intelligence to help you.

What follows is a list that I started and am handing over to you to add your creative space ideas to. My ideas are only there to ensure you have the essentials and hopefully to get you inspired. Now you can list all those things that will make your space feel amazing so that you're clear on what you need. Once complete, gather all the things on your list and put your creative space together today.

Creative Space List

- ◯ Inviting, quiet area to be alone in — NO devices.

- ◯ Soft window or warm lamp glow.

- ◯ Supportive seat at a table or on the floor.

- ◯ Simple art supplies.

- ◯ Optional — candle, drinking water, tea, etc.

- ◯

- ◯

- ◯

- ◯

- ◯

- ◯

- ◯

- ◯

Never Mind about Your Thinking Mind

Whenever we step into something new, there's a part of us that resists and clings to the familiar old ways. Remember the power of your thoughts here. As Henry Ford put it, "Whether you think you can or you think you can't—you're right."

Your Thinking Mind may be going into problem mode right about now, saying, "This is all a bit much. I don't know how to set up my creative space in my home." It's normal to feel this way. Tell that cautious Thinking Mind of yours to rest easy because for every problem, there are infinite creative solutions.

Here are some of the solutions that creative people have shared with me for handling hiccups around creating their special space.

- Form a pop-up creative space in the garage, at your dining room table, in an empty closet, or even in your back yard or a park if your home has limited space and lacks privacy. The art materials for each step are simple and few, so they can easily be carried with you and packed away in a box or basket when you're done.

- Time it well so that when you're in your creative space, others aren't around (e.g., kids are at school, early in the morning, late at night).

- If you're sharing a room for your designated creative space, then form a system to ensure you're undisturbed when you're using it (e.g., hang a "do not disturb" sign, tie a ribbon on the door handle).

Your Promise to Yourself

In order for you to experience what your Creative Intelligence can do for you, a quiet space is necessary—within and without. Unless you intentionally set up your space, with all the art materials you will need, you won't feel free to dive into the creative exercises up ahead. Each exercise lets you feel, experience, and literally see your innate creativity reflected back to you on the page while giving you information towards creating transformation in your life.

Words can't really describe what it's like to experience yourself this way. A deep sense of peace, acceptance, and love begins to grow as you uncover far more of who you are. I've felt it in myself and watched it countless times in those I have worked with, and it always takes my breath away.

We live such limited versions of ourselves in our routine-filled, day-to-day life. As you commit to creating this strong foundation, know that all the forces in the Universe will come to show you so much more of who you are!

Refresh and Review

- In order to truly create as the Creative Intelligence you are, it's essential to carve out inner and outer spaces of stillness, solitude, and quiet.

- As you prioritize peaceful solitude in your daily life, you will recharge your power and connect with Source to lift your vibration naturally.

- As you choose to focus upon something you want (Thinking Mind) and then feel it is already a part of your experience (Feeling Mind), you create a new vibration, which draws what you want to you through the Law of Attraction.

- Allow your own experiences of being in natural spaces that relax and uplift you inform you as you set up your creative space.

Creative Spark

Create Your Own Declaration

- Pick up your favorite colored marker and write on a piece of paper at least one thing that you will commit to doing today to set up your creative space (e.g., "I commit to gathering all the art materials from my children's supplies." Or, "I commit to clearing out the window-lit corner in the garage today."). Whatever the next step is for you, write it out clearly and commit to doing it today.

- Make it official and speak your words out loud, remembering you are the creator of your life and your words have power, starting with "Today I will commit to..."

- Sign and date your declaration and keep your word to set up your creative space before beginning the next chapter so that you are ready to transmit your unique colors through you as we continue on. It will be so worth your while!

In the next chapter, I will teach you how to creatively shift your stress right out of you with some warm-up exercises to activate your creative flow.

**Imagine this taking place for you now—
See it, feel it, be it!**

Chapter 4

Warm Things Up: Time to Play Your Way In

Welcome back! How did you enjoy setting up your creative space? Now you will have ample space in which to play. That's actually what this chapter is inviting you to do! It's time to play in a whole new way.

Do you remember the last time you played just for the fun of it? I don't mean the weekly ukulele or yoga class you're enrolled in either. While those are enjoyable, there's a scheduling and organization element that counters the spontaneity of free play. I'm asking about the curious and wonder-filled inclination for play that children in the great outdoors do naturally all day!

Whether climbing, hiding, building, or breaking things apart only to build something new, most children don't need to be told how to play. As you sit here now and imagine little ones going full out in their imaginal world, don't you sense yourself longing to join in? That's because there's a playful child tucked inside of you, and that child is ready to play now too!

If it's been a while and you need a reminder of how enjoyable it is to be this way, this chapter will take you there. Consider this your creative warm-up to prepare you for the seven steps for Creating a Life in Full Colors up ahead.

You're being invited to enjoy yourself. Let this release you from any fears you might have about drawing with colors on a page. You'll learn experientially how to follow your playful *pull* to the colors and shapes that attract you while learning how to handle your "inner nag," who may pop up time and again. Finally, you will see your unique colors start to flow through you onto your paper without any preconceived plan. Playing without a plan is something we rarely allow ourselves to do.

As you can likely sense, by the end of this chapter, you'll be feeling more playful than you may have felt in a long time. Aren't you curious to feel this buoyant shift within you? Then let's begin.

What This Might Bring Up for You

I wonder if you can guess what the biggest challenge is when I sit with someone for the first time and invite them to playfully ply their unique colors onto the paper. Any idea what it might be?

Perhaps it will help to imagine you are sitting with me now, side by side on floor cushions, legs criss-crossed like in grade school. Envision colored paper of almost every hue splayed out with an array of rainbow-colored chalk pastels on the floor between us. Got it? Wonderful!

Now…imagine I look into your eyes and ask you to play your unique colors out in any way that feels right for you. What would you feel inside if this invitation came to you right now?

For most people, this is far too much to ask. Especially if it's been a while since picking up a pastel, or any art supplies for that matter. This invitation can bring up so many things; a burning desire to dive straight into the colored pastels not being one of them.

The biggest obstacle here is a fear around "getting it right," which stems from our childhood conditioning. Many of us, including me, did not have positive creative experiences in our early years. More often than not, I hear people share with me that a voice of authority from their childhood—such as a teacher, parent, or even a coach—said or did something to give the clear signal that their unique expression was wrong in some way.

I remember a woman who didn't dare touch the colors initially in a workshop. Only later, after finding her way in, did she share the humiliation she felt as a little child in first grade when her teacher scolded her for painting her sky in a full array of rainbow colors. I remember another woman sharing how her grandmother reprimanded her so harshly for singing that she stopped sharing her expressive voice completely.

Such moments can be emotionally charged and can shut down our unique expression. It's important to acknowledge such moments if you have experienced them and notice the impact they have had upon your life.

Pause for a moment and reflect. When have you not dared to speak up or share your unique view for fear of being shut down or made wrong? Honor yourself for the memories that come up and for the transformation that you are now choosing for yourself.

If we retract from these shutdown moments, we lose an integral piece of who we are, and a nagging inner critic who keeps our expressive voice silent grows within. However, if you recognize that you can choose anew for yourself and step into your creative space now, saying, "I *get to* play today," you can move forward powerfully.

This act of playfully choosing *for* yourself has immense impact on what happens next here. In contrast, to choose from a place of "I should..." or "I've got to..." feels heavy and forced and will take all the joy out of (and likely even stop) your journey before you begin.

Creative One, go ahead, stand up tall in your creative space with me, stretch your hands up to the sky, and in the fullest, most expressive, unique voice say, "I *get to* play and unlock my creativity today!"

Beyond a creative warm-up, this is a whole new way of being really kind and easy on yourself. When we let the past be past and consciously choose to create a new way forward, we become far more playful and curious to discover more of who we are.

Little Ones Are Great Guides

Over the years, I have been fortunate to work with children of all ages from all parts of the world—from Japan to Bangkok to Dubai. More recently, I asked a young group to build whatever they wanted with empty cardboard boxes. As you can imagine, the results were imaginative and diverse, as boxes transformed into ships, farms, sprawling homes, and beyond! Besides being inspirational, the children's box creations also provided three important lessons for us all on how to play.

The first lesson is to follow your natural *pull* toward the things that attract you. When I offered the boxes to the children, they just knew which boxes were the right ones to use. The same for the art materials too. Whether they chose yarn, colored papers, textiles, feathers, or paint, they simply knew what they needed and chose without hesitation.

You also have this ability within you to follow your inner *pull* to choose very well for yourself. Both in art and in life. You likely don't even realize all the times each day that you're responding and choosing specific attractors in your life. Whether it's which clothes your wear each day or which chair to sit in at a cafe. As you begin to play with colors and art materials and scan through them, you'll become aware of the ones which attract and *pull* you as if to say, "Choose me!" Follow that hunch and choose accordingly.

Perhaps you've seen a child in an ice cream shop with their grandparents offering to buy them whatever flavor they want. You can be sure that the child is not thinking, *Oh, man, how annoying. Now I've got to choose from all of these flavors!* Not at all! They are simply in "I want this one!" mode as they point, grab, and lick away.

Trust yourself as you reach for that yellow crayon, even if you wouldn't usually choose that way. Take hold of the brush that seems to jump out at you, saying, "Take me!" Then twist it in curly spirals if that feels delicious to you. Drop that brush as soon as you're bored with it and pick up a crayon instead. Like that child grabbing their ice cream cone with certainty, your creative expressions will form with the various "flavors" and colors that attract you!

For fun, give this a try right now by walking through the rooms in your home, breathing deep into your heart as you go. From the heart space of your Feeling Mind, sense and notice which objects in your home seem to be drawing you to them; which ones attract you and *pull* your attention toward them like a magnet. Simply feel and make a note of them in the space provided for you here.

Notice if there's any connection between the objects you wrote down. Let's get playful with this, shall we? Using your imagination, ask your objects what they want to teach you right now. Listen in closely and enjoy what insights you receive. Then, be sure to write them down.

Give Your Inner Nag a New Gig

It all seems so simple, especially once you get into a momentum of feeling the energetic pull of an attractor and responding. Yet there's often an inner voice that can show up right when the childlike part of you is in full creative flow.

This brings us to the next important lesson; it's to recognize the arrival of your critical "inner nag," the nickname I use for this voice because it can go on and on if it's not redirected. It's helpful to learn how to give your inner nag a new gig so that it doesn't shut you down with its negative chatter.

Remember, you're in a new learning process, so your Thinking Mind might be in alert mode. This is new terrain, and your critical nagging voice will likely natter in your ear at some point to keep you from doing anything out of the ordinary. We humans are wired for patterns, and when we step out of the lines to try something new, there can be some kickback from within to try to stop us.

Think back to the children with their boxes. One boy's initial plan to build a treehouse village with his boxes didn't work out. This got his inner nag attacking him right away. Seeing the other children creating easily, he began to despair. When I asked him about it, he said, "I just can't do anything right! Everyone else is so far ahead of me now!" I told him about our critical inner nag voice and suggested he give his critical voice a job so it would leave him alone. He chose to send his inner nag to a nearby animal shelter to walk and play with all the pets and continued creating happily.

You too can send your inner nag out on errands or give it meaningful work, like telling it to clean up all the trash in the ocean. The mind doesn't know the difference between "real" and "imaginal" states, so have fun with this!

Knowing your critical inner voice will likely show up just as you dive into your playfulness, I invite you to list out all the new jobs for it to do ahead of time. Write down all the things that really need completing on a micro and macro scale. Set them down in the space provided so that you're fully prepared for that voice when it starts chattering. I put a few ideas down to get you started, but you need to complete the list so you can have it at the ready for when you need it.

Give Your INNER NAG A New Gig

- ✰ Save all the bees.
- ✰ Find lost pets.
- ✰ Mow the lawns of all the elderly in town.
- ✰
- ✰
- ✰
- ✰

Relax and Feel the Power of Play

Whenever we're learning something in a state of stress for fear of getting it wrong, our brains can't absorb the new information. This brings us to the third lesson in play. It's essential to be easy on yourself so that you can experience the joy of learning in a relaxed way. Haven't you noticed that you get the best learning from your challenges? So, embrace the perfection of imperfection and learn through every bump along the way!

Don't be afraid of looking silly or confused. We all have been there before. In my early days in Japan, I remember stopping by a convenience store to pick up a few things. I completely forgot how to say "eggs" in Japanese and couldn't find a dozen eggs anywhere so I decided to act like a chicken laying her eggs to show the staff what I was looking for. Only when a flustered employee brought me a special laxative drink did I realize how confusing my "request" must have been. To this day I remember that *tamago* means "egg" in Japanese!

As you let go of the idea that you need to "get it right" every time (as if there were ever such a thing as getting creativity "right") and allow everything to be as it is, you can drop straight into your heart and play in a free and curious way. If what we're focused upon is enjoyable and uplifting, we will naturally dive in with full engagement, both in our art and in our lives.

Isn't this what we all ultimately desire? When we attempt to map everything out and control life, we end up only partially engaged because our brain is so busy thinking ahead to the next thing that we can't be fully present.

When we release our grip on how things "should be," we can enter into pure discovery and access potentials we never imagined before. Sadly, we tend to dream too small for ourselves. Now is the time to let go and trust that there is great power in your playing. Know the Creative Intelligence within you is also the very same Divine Intelligence of the Universe. As you activate yours and they align, new possibilities will be evident to you.

All that's required of you is to set your intention to play like a child in full joy. Follow your *pull* to the colors that seem to light up for you, then allow the shapes and lines that feel good to you to flow onto the paper. Remember the preschool art filled with pure spontaneous expression I mentioned? With that in mind, why don't you give it a go in the space provided for you?

Simply choose the colors that attract you and experiment. What happens when you paint over an oily crayon or a pastel? What appears on the page when you hold three crayons and smudge them on their sides? What if you blend the chalks with your fingers and then tap the paper with your colorful fingertips? Go ahead—give it a go, and remember, if your inner nag gets noisy, quickly set it to work on its own project so that you can play in the quiet of your inner creative space.

Flower Power

How was that—to simply play with no plan? Were you able to really let go and explore with the art materials? Or did you keep in your "false control"? I know that sounds like a harsh statement, but I put it out there to help you as you move into the next phase of your journey ahead.

When I think of choosing to let go of "false control," my mind goes back to Ilona and the first time she came to the art studio to uncover more of her creative self. Though she entered the space looking serious and somewhat unsure, Ilona showed up willing to explore, just as you are learning to do here. The first day I met her, and each time she came to create, she gave herself full permission to play.

Watching Ilona trust herself and let go was moving for me. I could immediately see what a stretch it was for her. It is no small task to stand in front of a large paper taped to the wall in the far corner of a room, entering this experience blind, with no idea as to what might come through. And yet, even in that space of not knowing, Ilona played full out and let her Creative Intelligence come through.

On that day she plunged her brushes into colors to form rhythms, which danced around and around until she finally stepped back, tired and amazed. Shining back at her from her large paper on the wall was a ball of gold like the sun. The ball had petals, somewhat like a flower, which seemed to pulse with so much strength that none of us there in the studio could help but to stop and gaze.

If Ilona hadn't let go of the false idea that she needed to be "in control" for that first workshop experience, none of us would have experienced the beauty of her innate Creative Intelligence that day. She also wouldn't have had that chance to know herself in a whole new way as a highly creative being! Clearly, these colorful expressions that show up before us are reflecting the natural creators that we are back to us.

Your Chance to Choose Yourself First

The truth of the matter is that creative magic happens when we play without trying to control and plan out everything. Trust that the Creative Intelligence of the whole Universe longs to align and cocreate with you, and that can't happen if it's all preplanned and controlled by you. For this playful power to flow through you now and into the upcoming creative exercises, you need to stop gripping life's steering wheel and let Source be your copilot.

In truth, none of us really knows how everything is going to play out each moment. If you think you have full control, then think again. As I was trying to micromanage everyone and everything in my life, I found myself underground in an earthquake. Now, as I write this paragraph, the whole world is learning this lesson together as we walk through the global pandemic of COVID-19. I invite you to drop that sense of "false control" because it's just that: false.

What I do know is how you feel along the way is how you will feel when you arrive. So, take a moment for yourself and choose very well for your journey forward. Say it out loud or quietly in your beautiful heart with me now: "From here on in, *I get to* let my creative heart play out in ways that surprise and delight me!"

Refresh and Review

- In order to access your innate creativity, it's essential to form an inclination for childlike play. Nothing planned or organized, just a desire to enjoy yourself!

- This invitation to play can bring up resistance around "getting it right." Such resistance is common. You can change the whole energy of play for yourself by saying, "*I get to* play today!"

- Children are our best teachers on following their inner *pull,* and like them, you know instinctively what you're attracted to and can choose what lights you up.

- If your "inner nag" shows up to squelch your joy and enthusiasm while you're creating, simply redirect it and give that critical nagging voice a new gig.

- It's vital to be easy on yourself so that you can experience the joy of learning. Know that the Universe longs to cocreate with you, so let go of your "false control" and watch new colorful ways of being come through you.

Creative Spark

Create a Stress Ball Shift

- In the quiet of your creative space, take a moment to close your eyes and notice all the stress-filled thoughts taking up space in your head right now. Whether it's your growing to-do list, a worry about work, or a health concern, include them all.

- Set a piece of paper and your colored pastels or crayons in front of you so that they're easy to access. Sit comfortably and close your eyes if you're comfortable doing so. Breathe slowly and deeply. On each inhalation, imagine each stress-filled thought swirling together to form a ball of thoughts above your head. On each exhalation, see that ball of thoughts spiralling down your arm and out through your drawing hand.

- Open your eyes and choose the colors that attract you and form the lines, shapes, and doodles that express the stress and tension that you're feeling as you draw your ball of stress right out of you and onto your paper.

- Don't judge or analyze the lines and colors that show up. Send your "inner nag" off on a new gig should it start to chatter. There's no wrong or right here; simply move stress-filled energy out in scribbles, shapes, and fields of color. When you feel like your stress has fully shifted onto your drawing, the process is complete.

- Feel free to do whatever feels right to you with your drawing—crumple it up, tear it to pieces, fold it in half, or quietly thank it. You'll know what to do. Once you feel complete, let it go into the trash bin so you can move forward stress free!

Repeat this Creative Spark anytime you feel the need to shift stress out of your system! Feel free to share it with colleagues, friends, and family. It's a wonderful way to create a stress release and lighten up your energy.

**Imagine this taking place for yourself now—
See it, feel it, be it!**

A Little Breathing Space Before You Begin to Learn the 7 Steps

"We are a becoming…changing,
spiraling, transforming…We are sparks
of intelligence at play."

—Ann Mortifee

Now that you have designed a creative space for yourself and warmed up, it's time for a little breathing space before you journey further. With each step, you will receive more awareness while embracing all that is playing out before you—the highlights, lowlights, and everything in between.

Much like some artists who choose to create masterpieces with discarded, broken materials in order to transform them into something beautiful, you too can do the same thing with the seemingly damaged pieces of your life.

Even if you don't believe this is possible, aren't you curious about how to do this if it were? For now, just imagine that you could transform these broken pieces. That way, when anxiety hits you, or stress overwhelms you, or you buckle over in physical pain, you could know how to use these heavy moments for yourself rather than allow them to completely overtake you.

At this point, you may only have a small hunch of what your Creative Intelligence can do. By the end of this journey, it will be evident in and to you.

Take this all in now. Close your eyes for a moment as you breathe deeply into your heart and remind yourself that you have everything you need within to create a life of ease and joy. Even if you don't see it yet—like that upcycling artist in the process of creating something new—there's unlimited potential inside of you!

Notice what sensations move through you as you hold these thoughts in your heart. Are you sensing any colors, shapes, or rhythms in you? Pay attention to any words or phrases moving through your mind. Feel it all, and in the space provided, spill them out in your own colors. Let yourself express all that is going on within you and see in your artwork how far you have already come!

At the end of each chapter ahead, I will share more Creative Sparks with you to further ignite your activated Creative Intelligence. Each Creative Spark will bridge all that you learn here into your life in surprising and delightful ways! Please don't skip over them, as they are here for you to embody everything you learn along the way.

Enjoy playing your colors out, and when you're ready to Begin Within to create your Life in Full Colors, I'll be waiting in the next chapter for you.

The 7 Steps

"The way to get started is to quit talking and begin doing."

—Walt Disney

Chapter 5

Own It:
Your First Step to Creating a
Life in Full Colors

Here we are, Creative One, poised at the first step to Creating a Life in Full Colors.

Each of the upcoming seven steps will provide you useful tools for creating self-love and personal transformation out of the heavy-hued challenges in your life. Whether your heaviness is seemingly small, like a concern about a change in your friend's mood of late, or quite big, like a toxic work situation that is affecting your health, these all are challenges in different shades. Learning to respond to each of our various life challenges is an essential skill to master.

Change can only happen when we walk straight up to the very thing that is causing us pain, move into a place of responding rather than reacting, and claim it as our own. This is why the very first step for Creating a Life in full Colors from any and every challenge that you are experiencing is to Own It as your life's ultimate creative material.

In this chapter, we will look at the ways we fail to own our challenges. Perceiving obstacles strictly as sources of pain rather than opportunities for growth limits us. By owning the struggles that surface in our lives, our Creative Intelligence is revealed to us and changes the way we show up in the world. As we take responsibility for our heaviness and claim it as our own to create with, things can take on a new trajectory. Even when the heaviness we're walking through is unclear, our Creative Intelligence comes through for us the moment we take this first step.

Cave to Self-Discovery

Think about a time in your life where you were moving through your days with nothing on the surface seemingly out of place yet all the while, a greater part of you could detect a sort of discord beneath the activity of your life.

When I first met Naoko, a young mother of a three-year-old son, she was going through such a phase. She asked me to hold a creative workshop for the mothers in the community and approached me with such an urgency in her big brown eyes that I knew it was vital to follow through.

A week or so later, the morning workshop was on. Naoko and several young mothers settled in and began expressing themselves with various art materials. Within the first hour, bright, colored artwork began filling the sunlit multi-purpose room. A strong contrast to Naoko's painting.

I watched Naoko that morning sitting cross-legged on the floor in front of a huge piece of paper about two meters wide and one meter tall. She had cut and taped this vast white void horizontally on the wall space in front of her. Naoko kept herself busy in the paints, all of which turned dark umber and gray as they mixed and blended into her painting. With quiet concern, she discovered after some time that she had painted herself into a large, dark, cave-like hole. This wasn't easy for her to sit with, considering all the lighter artwork in the space around her.

However, when the cave image surfaced on her paper, Naoko didn't pretty it up with colorful paints or try to bury it by overlaying brighter colors on top of it. She "owned it." She took responsibility for her cave, recognizing pieces of her life echoing the heaviness of its dark gray stone.

Her artwork motivated her to take intentional steps into self-discovery and personal exploration. She decided to work further with me, beyond the workshop, as she faced and owned her painting, wondering, *What is hidden in there? Is it time to go inside?* and, finally, *What might I discover as I journey in?*

From Reactivity to Receptivity

Naoko is not alone. We all are looking for ways to reconcile with the deepest, darkest pieces of ourselves, to transform ourselves, and to create a fully integrated life. The impulse we have to run from our deeper feelings results in us not responding to our innermost truths. All too often, we aren't patient enough to learn from such moments; we want to problem solve pain rather than keep company with it. Our knee-jerk response is reactivity—we can easily become accusatory and judgmental.

If you notice yourself playing the role of judge, not wanting to dig in to uncover and own what heaviness may be hidden underneath your reactivity, you are not alone. In judge mode we begin shaming and blaming people, events, circumstances, even ourselves, rather than owning our pain and responding to it.

In fact, our animal nature is wired with a fight-flight-or-freeze response to react whenever we sense a threat around us. We know we are far more than our animal nature. Now that we are awakened to the Creative Intelligence that we are, we can exercise our choice to respond in a more expansive and loving way.

By shaming and blaming others and ourselves, we close our hearts and begin to lose access to our interconnectedness and aliveness. When we shut down our hearts, everything around us fills in on the surface layer of our lives, quite like when we fill in a coloring-book page. While it's possible to color all the shapes perfectly, it's still a surface image that only pulls our focus outwardly.

When we avoid feeling our pain, we actually create and bring more painful experiences toward us. This only brings more reactivity. Please, don't settle for a shallow coloring-book life. You have so much more within the depths of you to explore and share with the world.

I invite you to create some awareness around where you may be denying and reacting to important challenge-filled creative materials for you. Pick up a pen, and with your non-writing hand on your heart, focus your breath into your heart center. As you breathe into your heart, write down all the people and events that you have judged as wrong and closed yourself off from in the space provided.

Acknowledge everyone and everything that came through your awareness and onto the page as an important part of your journey. Own your connection to them without trying to fix your challenges with them or sort out what to do next. Just sit and be with each one in quiet curiosity as Naoko was in the discovery of her unexpected cave.

The power of the heart is the power that fuels us to create a meaningful life in which we can leverage all of our pain-filled moments and create them anew. This is not to say that you should gloss over painful events; however, when you are ready and receptive to own your pain as a portal to healing, rather than a spiral downward to defeat, you will move from victimhood into your powerful creative strength.

While this is not at all the easy way, we are given the choice within each challenge we face to own our pain and heaviness. Why is owning it so essential? It's because there is always intelligence and wisdom embedded within our suffering, waiting for us to take hold of it. Our challenges break us open wide to discover something new that's hidden inside.

Remember to Remain Curious

What I'm inviting you to do might feel almost impossible to you, especially if you have never chosen to dig into your heavy-hued challenges before. It can feel like it's too much to ask. I want to remind you of the importance of remaining curious in all of this. Childlike, openhearted inquiry is not the same as childish tantrums and acting out, by the way.

Go slow now; this is the first step of seven coming new to you. Don't rush the process. Trust in your own timing. It may also be too much at this point to see your challenges as gifts to unwrap instead of painful parts to avoid. Honor your own timing and go at your own pace.

Do you remember when we started this journey together and I shared with you my dark moment which transformed into my miracle moment of awakening? I wonder if you recall my therapist's words about the mobile hanging from the ceiling; that when one piece is touched, all the pieces move and change. Like her, I can say wholeheartedly to you that if you are faithful to yourself, things can indeed change for you and, in turn, for all the people around you if you choose to own your heavy pieces going forward from today.

Remember that I'm with you here, and all the forces in the Universe are rushing to meet you too. To choose this inward journey of healing and creating life anew is not a little thing. You're now choosing to cocreate with Creator, and there is great power in this decision.

Allow expectation to move right through your whole being and let it propel you forward into the upcoming Creative Spark at the end of this chapter. I'll open the space for you to lay all your current challenges down in front of you, big and small, one and the same. Just like the mobile, you will discover precisely which piece to make contact with as you Own It so that everything can shift.

When the Waves Roll In

Before you head off into the quiet of your creative space, I want to share Rebecca's story with you. Rebecca's first experience with Creating Healing began precisely at this "Own It" step.

When Rebecca and I first met while paddle boarding in a group in Dubai, she was plunging into a sudden transition. With two small children and a husband soon heading off to begin a new job in Europe, Rebecca was experiencing enormous stress. Add to this the huge task of packing up her home and saying goodbye to her friends and life in Dubai on a very tight schedule, and the stress only amplified.

What's more, Rebecca was moving with her children to her hometown in the United States after many years abroad. This meant squeezing into her mom's home so that she could complete the practicum portion of her master's degree. I know; it's a lot to take in! I'm exhausted just writing it all down. Can you imagine how Rebecca was feeling?

Besides being utterly wearied, Rebecca also felt as if she was being pulled in several directions. She shared her struggles as we paddled out on a swelling sea, upon which Rebecca struggled to find her balance and fell more than once. It was as though her paddle boarding was mirroring the difficulty she was having in finding the balance she desperately needed at such an intense time of transition.

A few days later, we met for a session. I shared with her how every storm has an eye within the center that is completely calm. We humans are no different; when everything is whirling around us, if we stop to quiet into our breath for even a moment or two, we can find our calm center.

While in the moment it seems like the last thing we should do, in times of overwhelming challenges, it's best to stop, do nothing for a while, and breathe deep into the heart. I guided Rebecca to shut her eyes, breathe deep, and focus inside, then invited her to flow her turbulent overwhelm out onto the page in front of her.

Rebecca wrote down each challenge and pain point, mapping her life situation onto paper, which she nearly filled from top to bottom. At first, seeing everything laid out before her brought tears to her eyes. It can be quite shocking to see all the challenges we are carrying around with us fully visible this way.

I shared how everything that she wrote down would shift as she owned it as hers to work with. Rebecca did just that. She listened to her strong inner voice to guide her as I invited her to own all of her challenges and to uncover which challenge was ready to shift. After getting her answer, I asked her to create something totally new: to cut shapes into her challenge-filled page, then use the various pieces for a whole new piece.

Reflecting later, Rebecca described her experience: "I used the scissors to recreate my image of a beautiful day with fish in the sea, birds in the air, and coconuts in the trees among the warm sun shining down on us all. When I looked at my picture, I didn't see all the anger, confusion, frustration, and worry; but I saw life. All my dark pieces were turning into living things."

And with that, her life's mobile shifted! As she created the new piece, she received clear guidance from her innate Creative Intelligence for what to do next. Rebecca became aware that she needed to first focus on getting her home organized and cleaned out. Simple, effective, and clear like her new artwork. The Universe is wise that way, giving us an intelligent "next step" to take from our challenge the moment we Own It and tune into what our heart has to say.

Your Chance to Let Your Heart Help You

Remember, we've already seen how the heart informs the brain far more than the brain does the heart. If you do not trust this first step and ignore the guidance of your heart, then you will not know which challenge is asking you to Own It in order to create healing for yourself now.

By trusting your powerful heart, you can access clarity to move forward in strength. The more you do this, the easier it becomes to own your challenges for the learning they hold. We can't see tomorrow, but our Source can, as it guides and supports us forward each step of the way.

As you continue in your heart, synchronistic events will start to happen for you. It's like a filter drops away, and we open up to a whole new way of being human, noticing that miracles are all around us! We end up following a nudge to end up at the right place at the right time. Minutes, hours, or even days ahead, our Creative Intelligence can guide us toward doing, or not doing, something, bring us synchronous events, and give us discernment and the clarity we so need.

Now, I'm getting ahead of myself here, but it's hard to contain my enthusiasm for what these seven steps will bring to your life. For now, it's essential that you master this first step very well for yourself. Make a decision to respond rather than react to your unique challenge and to Own It, knowing it is the starting point for you to create a Life in Full Colors for yourself.

Refresh and Review

- All too often we follow the impulse to avoid our challenges, which limits us from receiving the rich wisdom they hold.

- Reacting to our challenges can make us judgmental—shaming and blaming ourselves or others for our situations. This closes our hearts, which limits our interconnectedness with all of life.

- When we are receptive and see pain as a portal to healing, we shift from victimhood to being the creator of our powerful healing story.

- When overwhelmed, remember that the heart is wise and knows the one painful piece that needs to shift for everything to follow naturally like a mobile in motion.

Creative Spark - Step 1

Own It
Your Creative
Mobile Map

- In the quiet of your creative space, sit with a piece of paper, colored crayons, markers, or pastels. Close your eyes and bring your breath into your heart. Inhale for five seconds and exhale for five seconds. Repeat until you feel calm.

- Choose the colors that attract you and draw an aerial-view drawing of a wire mobile to form a creative mind map. Do this by drawing a circle the size of your fist in the middle of your paper; then draw several lines outwardly like the rays of the sun to represent your mobile's wires.

- Imagine you're able to take an aerial-view of your life and look at all of your challenges—big and small—that you currently are experiencing.

They may range from an unfinished list of things to do, to feeling exhausted at home with small children, to a medical concern, or maybe there's a conflict at work that seems unsolvable. Without judging or engaging with them, write each challenge on its own line radiating out from the inner circle. If you feel you need more lines to hold more challenges that come to mind, simply draw in more.

- If a certain color or symbol for your challenges is attracting you, include it; fill up your mobile with the words and colors that express your current struggles most accurately for you.

- Once you have set your current challenges out onto your paper, stand up to get a higher view and notice what feelings you experience. Are you overwhelmed and moved to tears like Rebecca was? Are you feeling lighter with this new perspective? Note and express exactly what you're feeling inside the circle using lines, scribbles, shapes, words, or symbols that feel right to you. All challenges and emotions are valid here. Don't judge them; simply let them be and own them!

- Set your hands on your heart to activate your heart's Creative Intelligence as you ask, "Which of these challenges is the one to own right now?"

Scan your whole mobile map and notice which challenge has the most charge to it. Take your time here, as this is a new way of being with your heaviness. There will be one that feels like it's lit up for you and attracting you. Notice that! Let your Creative Intelligence surprise you here; it usually isn't the challenge your Thinking Mind selects. Trust your Feeling Mind, as it knows the one piece of the mobile that's ready to shift.

- Once it's clear which challenge is the one for you to focus on, circle it or highlight it with a color. Turn your paper over, write it down, and speak out loud what you are owning right now. You might write: "I own my lower back pain right now," or "I own my financial debt right now."

Celebrate your challenge because as you Own It, it will shift your whole life mobile as you take it forward into the second step of Creating a Life in Full Colors.

**Imagine this taking place for yourself now—
See it, feel it, be it!**

Chapter 6

Ask on It:
Your Second Step to Creating a
Life in Full Colors

*D*o you remember me telling you about the therapist I met just before my miracle moment? The wise woman who told me to "turn everything upside down"? Her words took on significance not only as I found myself underground during the earthquake but also in my first week of training as an art therapist. Our instructor asked us to locate a unique attractor object to help us answer some big questions on our struggles.

I went looking for a long time, empty-handed, when I grew tired and stopped to sit down on a sturdy flat rock beside the sea. Turning my gaze toward where the shore meets the water, I saw it immediately. A clear marble with the midmorning sun bouncing off it as if to beckon me. Picking it up, I examined its scuffed surface and unique swirl of cloudy glass inside before asking it the questions my instructor gave me. The final question was: "What have you to teach me about my suffering?"

As I asked this, I followed a sudden impulse to peer through the marble into the scene right in front of me. Squinting through the glass, I saw everything—the beach, the sky, and the sea—turned completely upside down.

With a shiver through my whole body, something clicked deep within me. I realized how exquisitely everything—especially my life's most challenging parts—had come together precisely for this upside-down moment to teach me a higher way of perceiving and relating to my struggles. They are here to peer into as portals to potentials that our eyes can't yet see. They're here to be looked at upside down, not as problems but opportunities.

As you look at challenges in this whole new way, it's my intent that, through this chapter, you will come to know the power that asking the right question of your challenges can open up for you. You will also uncover why this won't happen until you decide to stop retelling your past story.

Like a curious scientist, you will learn to create a new experience for yourself by upping your current level of perception. Together we'll build upon Einstein's well-known observance: "Problems cannot be solved by the same level of thinking that created them." You will learn how to live less as the solid, stuck, struggle-filled version of you and transform into the wisdom-filled wave of energy within the Unified Field.

Sound interesting enough for you? Maybe even a little bit magical and mystical too? Wonderful! That's the way it should feel. Remain as open as possible because this chapter will teach you how to Ask on your challenges in a whole new way!

Hello, Possibility!

Have you ever known someone who when faced with a challenge receives it like an intriguing visitor at their doorway? Opening the door wide to add it to their ever-expanding experience of life? I think of my dad, with an inquisitive engineering mind, welcoming all "in need of repair" situations.

I remember growing up, sheepishly presenting Dad with various items that I had broken—a bed board cracked from jumping on it, a bike frame bent from a crash, even a crumpled bumper on the family car. I also remember the relief within me when Dad's face would shift from concern to intentional focus on finding a solution.

This ability to welcome in challenges with curiosity for uncovering what hidden potentials they hold is within everyone. Far beyond broken bikes and bed frames, you have the capacity within you to greet each challenge that comes to visit you expectantly.

Now, let's be real here; this doesn't mean you won't ever have a reaction to your challenges. In fact, it's well within your natural stress response to react. But that reaction time should not last for more than a few minutes. Any reactivity that lingers is not helpful to your health and happiness.

Sadly, staying stuck in reactivity with no clue how to return to your relaxed center has become the norm for many. How can we connect with our Higher Power in such moments? How do we turn towards and ask the right questions of our challenge when it shows up? We're going to explore that right now.

The Ultimate Do-Over

The first thing to be aware of is what a wonderful gift you are giving yourself when you choose to respond with inner calm to a situation. Choosing to reframe a challenge provides you with a fresh opportunity to release a heavy version of your life story to create it anew.

As you move forward, it's important to see that how you choose to think, feel, and talk about your challenge is how you will experience it. Remember, we create from our level of thought, so becoming aware of our thoughts and how they make us feel as they form into the words we speak provides an opening for us to create new way of being.

Not everyone jumps at this opportunity, of course. Many get stuck in a place I call "moan and groan." Even those who come to me in all earnestness, saying, "Corry, I really am tired of my back pain/bad marriage/endless sadness/etc., and want to heal," are stuck here. Unfortunately, they miss out on their opportunity to transform their challenge by refusing to release their habit of moaning and groaning about their situation.

We all know what it feels like to be stuck there; when we're in so much pain, and all we want to do is tell everyone around us all about it! This doesn't help anyone within earshot of you. It also forms an internal loop of "woe is me" within your brain too. I should know—mine looped for decades, and I still have to keep this old habit in check!

When we're stuck in this zone of "moan and groan," it's simply because we have bought into the idea that incessant talking about our pain is the best way to deal with it. In reality, you end up creating more to complain about! Law of Attraction does not discriminate; it simply gives us more of what we're giving our attention to, including our suffering.

While it can feel good in the moment to dump our stuff on another, we end up feeling worse afterward, having not changed our circumstances while draining those around us. Ultimately, we're all energy, and only when we choose to lighten up and stop the steady stream of "woe is me" can a new approach be made.

We can begin to transform and upcycle our challenge the moment we choose to quiet down and turn our attention inwardly. With this new focus, we instantly drop the role we were playing of the "victim" crying out, "Why did this happen to me?" to play the part of the "curious explorer," wide open to possibilities, surprises, and new discoveries. This is the ultimate do-over that each of us is entitled to!

I invite you to drop all the things you tend to hear yourself moan and groan about in the space provided. As you write them out and let them go, feel your energy lighten and your spine straighten. It feels so good to rise after you release all these heavy complaints!

Time to Level Up

While we all have full access to the Divine Spaciousness within us, most of us don't consider entering in. If we're bound up by troubles in our outer world, accessing the Universe within us sounds utterly impossible and downright useless. For many, the reply to such an unconventional invitation is: "What?! You're asking me to turn inwardly when I have all this stuff falling apart in my life?"

Until we approach problems and challenges as the Creative Intelligence we are, we remain stuck indefinitely. We end up hammering at a problem like a woodpecker going full force on a tree. If our inner space remains unexplored, our focus only narrows, leaving us stuck for months, years, even a lifetime. This then hinders us from seeing possibilities that are sitting right in front of us.

We're now living in a remarkable time where new science is revealing what the mystics and ancients have always known. We are not these solid-looking forms running around in jeans and T-shirts that we appear to be. We are highly complex vibrations of Universal light and Intelligence within the Unified Field.

This Unified Field is an invisible field of vast energy connected to everything and every possibility for the highest benefit of all. It exists outside of the limitations of linear time and space that we experience here in the material 3-D world. We can't see it with our human eyes, but it can be felt; it's purely energetic. If it seems my words are limited and unable to describe it, that's because you can't truly *know* it without unfolding *as it*.

Which of our minds gives us access to the Unified Field then? While the Thinking Mind is essential for learning, analyzing, and navigating decisions, none of these tools provide access. In fact, the brain scans of meditators taken while in the Unified Field reflect the slow flow brain waves found in alpha and theta states. Beta brain waves, which are indicative of the Thinking Mind, just can't take you there. This means we must slow our brain waves down and unfold into the field from the Feeling Mind.

Once again, the best guides are...you guessed it...children immersed in imaginative play. Have you ever watched a child dress up as their favorite superhero? They completely forget their whole identity outside of their superpowers and superhero costume. They believe that they truly *are* the super-hero they are emulating.

We enter the Unified Field in a very similar way, substituting the superhero suit for the vast, loving, infinite spaciousness of the Universe instead. To enter and unfold *as it*—the Unified Field—*it* is what you must become.

Why not get a sense of this unfolding of yourself as the field now? After you read the instructions below, quietly close your eyes and shift your focus away from all you think yourself to be. Drop every-thing you consider to be you. Peel off all of your layers of identity—your name, your nationality, your occupation, your gender, your relationship to others (wife, husband, daughter, father, uncle, sister, etc.), your personality type, and so on.

Keeping your awareness in your heart, slow down your breath; lengthen your inhalation, hold, and extend your exhalation to twice as long as your in-breath. Bring an elevated feeling of love, joy, and compassion into your heart center, expanding your awareness with each breath. Feel your energy merge into the formless and timeless void of the Universe. Bask without thought in the void of the Unified Field and linger for as long as you desire. Sense and feel the subtle softening of energy in and around you.

Though it sounds simple to "feel it and become it," much discipline and practice is needed here, as your Thinking Mind will get agitated and start reminding you "who you are." Its job is to keep things humming along as always, so with you venturing into timeless and formless terrain, it will natter loudly to bring you back to what it thinks is "normal." Keep trying; it will learn to listen to your direction as you visit the field again and again.

While that was just a little taste for you to experience the Unified Field, there are many guided meditations and teachings available on YouTube for accessing and understanding more. I highly recommend the videos by neuroscientist Dr. Joe Dispenza to deepen this work for you. The Creative Spark at the end of this chapter will provide you another opportunity to Ask on your challenge from the field, beyond time and space.

Now, Ask from Here

By now, it should be quite clear that when you're asking higher questions from your loving heart, you are in complete alignment with the Universe. By activating your Feeling Heart, you are creating heart coherence, which provides access to infinite potentials and possibilities.

This is very different from asking from a stress-filled, high-beta-wave mind, which has no access to the field. In fact, when we feel cut off from our Source, we can forget that the support of the Whole Unified Field even exists! That's when our focus narrows, and in our perceived helplessness we ask, "Why me?!"

With an expansive, intentional practice of connecting with Universal Intelligence, you can relax, knowing that you are collaborating with all of life. This takes the enormous weight of "figuring things out myself" right off of your shoulders. Asking from the heart means you can expect to receive loving guidance, wisdom, and synchronous events from Source to work in your favor.

Entering the field, Ask higher questions of your challenge, either loudly or in silence energetically:

"What might I discover through this?"

"What if you were ultimately a gift?"

As these powerful questions reverberate out, know your intentional vibrations are holding you and your challenge within that loving Universal Vastness of the field with infinite intelligence and information. Your questions could not have formed if the answers were not already there and on their way to surfacing for you. Perhaps you can sense into the responses already, or maybe you need a little more time.

There's no need to rush the process. You already have your responses within you, whether you sense them or not. You will learn how to access them with ease in the next chapter. For now, sit back and enjoy the anticipation. In fact, why not pause and get yourself a cup of tea, as I have someone special I want to introduce you to. Someone who inspired me with how he chose to Ask on his life challenges from a very young age.

I'd Like You to Meet Sean

When Sean Stephenson was born, doctors told his parents not to expect their newborn son to live for more than twenty-four hours. Born with brittle bone disease, Sean defied all of the doctors' predictions, living life full out in strength and joy until his fortieth year, in spite of numerous challenges and constant physical pain.

Dependent upon his wheelchair to get around and requiring support to get dressed and bathed each day, Sean never saw himself as needy or weak. Sean lived a full life as a therapist, a loving husband, and as an inspirational speaker to countless people. Throughout his life, Sean generously shared his humor, his wisdom, and his purpose, which was to help rid people of insecurity and to fill them up with love instead.

While I never met Sean personally, I learned so much from him through what he shared in his *TEDx Talk* and his social media posts. I especially loved how he embraced each challenge in his life however it showed up. He developed this resilience when he was only ten years old and found himself in anguish after a fall resulted in an excruciating break to his femur bone. Raging at his situation and in despair at his condition, he cried out, "What did I do to deserve this?"

That's when his mom, rushing to his side to help him, looked him in the eye and asked, "Sweetie, is this going to be a gift or a burden in your life?" Sean said that question changed everything for him that day.

Sean had received all kinds of gifts before, but up until his mom asked him that higher question, he never imagined that a gift could show up in such a painful way. And yet, something within him rose up to a place within where he could receive and honor the gift of his challenge fully. Sean recognized that his whole life could be a gift to humanity because everyone experiences pain in their own way.

For Sean, knowing the purpose of your pain doesn't remove it; rather, it keeps you present and engaged with life. Before Sean left this earth, he honored the purpose that the right question revealed to him that painful day. He lived full out from his heart, engaging with people in the midst of their pain to remind them of their power to choose their way through it.

Like Sean, you have the power within you to shift from crying out in pain to asking what your challenge can gift you. For this to work, you have to let your powerless story fall away. As you know now, to receive answers from the Universe, it's essential to focus into your heart space while releasing your habit of overidentifying with your small self. This is your opportunity to merge into the Loving Source of life that you are!

Failing to do this will keep you stuck somewhere similar to where Sean was, crying out angrily. We've all been there, and while it serves as an essential point in our journeys, it's not where we want to remain. After you refresh and review, I invite you to step into the quiet of your Creative Space. From there, you can experience your next Creative Spark, which will expand you out into the loving, intelligent Unified Field, which holds you and all your questions willingly. I'll meet you there.

Refresh and Review

- Your life journey can turn completely around when you begin to see your personal challenges as portals for undiscovered potentials.

- Allowing challenges to enter your life with awareness provides you the ability to Ask higher questions of them.

- Most of us have been conditioned to "moan and groan" outwardly to others and inwardly to ourselves about our struggles, which can leave us stuck.

- The combination of shifting the focus away from all that we identify with while heightening feelings of love within the heart to expand out as pure awareness is the way to enter the Unified Field.

- By dropping the powerless "Why me?" question and instead asking, "What might I discover through this?" and "What if you were ultimately a gift?", you can fully expect to receive an intelligent response from Source.

Creative Spark - Step 2

Ask on It
Creating in the Unified Field

- In the quiet of your creative space, lay your colored crayons and paper in front of you. Set your Creative Mobile Map from the last Creative Spark nearby with the "I own_____" statement side facing up and clearly visible to you. Reconnect with this special challenge, as it is your ultimate art material which you will be upcycling through each of the seven steps.

- Write the following statements at the top of your paper; then speak them out loud:

  1. I AM cocreating with the Universe
  2. I AM asking my challenge, "What might I discover through this?" and "What if you were ultimately a gift?"
  3. I AM receiving wisdom and intelligence now.

- With one hand on your heart and the other on your paper, begin to breathe deeply for five seconds, imagining energy flowing powerfully into your heart center. Hold this breath for five seconds, then exhale for eight seconds. This will help slow and deepen your breath. Repeat this process eight times.

- As you breathe, invite an elevated feeling of love, joy, and compassion into your heart center, expanding your awareness with each breath. Feel your energy merge into the formless and timeless void of the Universe. Bask without thought as the void of the Unified Field. Sense in and feel the subtle lightening of energy in and around you.

- Without breaking your relaxed state, slightly open your eyes to halfway, to a gentle squint, and begin to doodle playfully onto your paper with your handwriting. Trust that the colors intended for this drawing will come easily to your hand while you create in the Universal Vastness without planning or thinking.

- Let your colors move and change with your slow breath. Do what feels good to you and focus on the elevated emotions within your heart. Trust the Universe to move through you, aligning your breath, movement, and heart.

- Stay in this moving meditation for as long as you desire. You are playing in the Unified Field of Intelligence, and the questions you put out to the field are now activating an expressive response. Don't rush this or minimize the power of playing in the field this way. Enjoy calming and energizing your system while accessing new possibilities.

- When you feel complete, open your eyes fully with wonder and curiosity. Stay out of analysis. This seemingly primitive drawing holds immense Creative Intelligence, which you will learn to receive insights from in the next chapter.

Put your drawing in a safe and private place (away from the eyes that don't understand its significance), as you will need it for your next Creative Spark. Well done. You just received a Creative Intelligence download from the Unified Field!

**Imagine this taking place for yourself now—
See it, feel it, be it!**

Chapter 7

Receive from It:
Your Third Step to Creating a
Life in Full Colors

Here we are, Creative One, at the cusp of step three. Well done for coming this far and for deepening your experience of your Creative Intelligence by owning and asking on your challenge. You are likely deepening your awareness through each Creative Spark of how you and the Universe are one and the same. It's my hope that you come to know tangibly that the energy which flows out in the Unified Field is the same stuff of life flowing within your precious form too.

In spite of initial appearances, there are a whole lot of gifts to receive from your challenge. This next "Receive from It" step is for you to learn how to do this very well. Isn't that worth celebrating? Then why don't we? C'mon, stand up real tall in a star shape—feet wide and arms outstretched. Now wrap yourself up in a big warm hug as you tip your head back and feel yourself smile. Doesn't that feel amazing? Could you receive all the love within your hug?

For many, receiving in any shape or form (be it a compliment, moral support, or even a promotion at work) can be a difficult if not seemingly impossible thing to do. I say seemingly because it's always possible to learn how to receive. Sometimes we just need a little help along the way. When we allow ourselves to open wide and receive, we can access the Divine's loving abundance that streams to us.

Much Love and Miracles

While we're talking about this loving abundance, why don't we start things off with a love story? Don't you just love a love story? I sure do! Especially those magical ones that develop slowly over the years like this one.

When Sam and Allan met for the first time twenty years ago, there was a warm respect felt by both. Over time, each left Africa to live and work overseas; Sam moved to the Middle East, and Allan made his way to Europe before the Universe would dovetail them back together again.

Allan's sudden reappearance, initially through texts, felt divinely timed to Sam, who had put out a request to the Universe for a spiritually connected life partner after her own recent awakening. Though Allan was nothing like the previous men in Sam's life, she sensed this was a good sign, as she was aware of the need for a change in the pattern.

It was at this point of their love story that Sam came to me for a Creating Healing session. She wanted clarity around her progressing relationship with Allan. Sam received clarity and so much more when her mother's spirit, in the form of a ruby-red-colored butterfly, showed up quite mystically in Sam's painting.

I had invited Sam to paint a feeling-based painting of what she wanted to receive and experience in her life. Initially, the painting surfaced a man and a woman standing close together. Suddenly, a butterfly appeared, alighting on the woman's shoulder before it began to expand. Finally, it grew so big that its wings enveloped both figures like a warm embrace.

Sam shared afterward that her mother, who died twenty years ago, had known and liked Allan very much. It meant the world to Sam that Allan and her mother had a warm bond. Butterflies had always connected Sam to her mother, so for one to appear in her spontaneous painting so prominently was, to Sam, her mother's spirit fully blessing the couple. In addition to this sacred visit, Sam got clarity, which opened her heart to trust that she could receive Allan's love.

As we completed Sam's session with an energy healing, she shared how waves of loving frequencies pulsed through her heart as it was opened wider still. With Sam's heart coherence so high, it didn't surprise me to learn that during her drive home, Allan suddenly called her from Europe. The Universe does all the coordinating when we are aligned with it. With Sam wide open to trust and receive Allan's love, the pair moved seamlessly forward into a loving relationship.

This love story touches something deep within us as it reminds us we can always make the vulnerable choice to let love in. This choice, as Sam shared, "does not come naturally because receiving is a vulnerable thing." To receive unconditional love, whether from a person or the Universe itself, requires vulnerability.

Each of us has experienced the helplessness felt in vulnerability during challenging moments in our lives. When such heavy moments arise, we can use the opportunity to stay open in spite of our fear. We always have the option to Own, Ask, and Receive from our challenging moments and to step toward them rather than close up or run away.

Those who make that higher choice of meeting their challenges are rewarded in so many ways. It's no wonder that one of the most popular *Ted Talks* of all time is Brené Brown's talk on vulnerability. In fact, I encourage you to take a few minutes to watch it on YouTube, as it's filled with more gems for you than I have the space to mention here.

It's Trickier than You'd Think

What about when you want to open your heart, but it seems to be stuck? What is stopping you from receiving in such moments? Sam spoke wisely to this as well. "By default I'm a giver! I give and I give to help others—family, friends, even people I don't know. Receiving is so heavy on me; I push back and react and say 'no.' It does not come naturally for me. It's something I'm discovering still, and I believe that's what Allan is here to teach me...to receive."

Being able to receive is a gift to others, ultimately, because when we receive, we give others the gift of giving. Deepak Chopra puts it simply: "Giving and receiving are different expressions of the same flow of energy in the universe."

Turn your attention back to the challenge you are learning to upcycle. Whether it's related to your relationship (love or other), career, health, or anything else under the sun is of no matter. What's important is to recognize your unique challenge is inviting you to receive abundantly from it. The question is, are you in balance to let it all in?

Sam came to realize that part of her life journey is to learn to balance her yin and yang energies. These are the two polarities of life that are within each one of us, woman or man—yin being the softer, feminine, and holding (receiving) energy, and yang being the harder, masculine, and activating (giving) energy.

For Sam, the years of living alone, taking care of herself while building her corporate career, resulted in her yang energy growing more dominant. Looking back, she could see that when previous partners had tried to take care of her, she couldn't receive. Even a simple gesture, like helping her with her coat, would trigger her to respond, "No, no, really, I'm fine," turning the caring gift away.

Only when Sam began to awaken to Creator's unconditional love within her did her growing awareness reveal a need to balance her yin and yang energy. As she left corporate life to turn her focus inwardly, not only did she bring more balance to her energies, but she also attracted Allan into her life, not surprisingly.

How about your yin and yang energies? What does your balance between receiving and giving look like? Curious to find out? All you need are some colored markers as you spend a few minutes in your quiet creative space, reflecting upon the ways you give and receive.

Perhaps you freely give compliments but can't receive them. Maybe you're able to take suggestions and advice, yet you're not able to voice your thoughts to others. Also notice where you're very balanced. It could be that you're as comfortable giving a hug as receiving one. Without overthinking it, close your eyes and take three slow, deep breaths and then write whatever comes through you. Color in and doodle as you feel inspired in the space provided for you here. Trust that the necessary information will flow out.

Receptive
Yin Energy

Active
Yang Energy

Strength in Stillness

How was it to creatively explore your giving and receiving balance? While it might seem like a simplistic process, you can receive many insights as you write and reflect this way. Research shows that when you take a few moments to still yourself and put pen to paper, you fire and wire a hundred times more neurons in your brain than when you sit and simply think it through.

Let's take a closer look here at stillness. If you think about it, stillness is readily available to you in all the "in-between" moments you spend waiting. All those perceived interruptions, like waiting in line at the supermarket or being stuck in a traffic jam, are perfect access points for stillness if you choose to engage with them that way.

We can leverage all of these moments spent waiting as opportunities to cocreate with the Divine and transform the energy within us and all around us. When I forget this option is available to me, I tend to be in a state of frustration, trying hard to get everything done by myself, completely missing the steady support of Source within the stillness of waiting.

Remember, you've already asked the Universe higher questions of your challenge. Now expect to receive in any which way. The gifts coming to you can only be experienced and enjoyed if you can get still enough to let them through. This takes practice, of course, but with so many "in-between" moments coming your way each day, you won't lack for opportunities to give it a go.

Practicing stillness makes me think of a podcast about nonresistance I heard a few years back. The host spoke about a traffic light near her home that was red almost every time she approached it. The light felt frustratingly long for her until she suddenly became aware that she could welcome the moment of stillness it provided her and use the time and space to focus on all she was thankful for.

With this new approach, she grew to enjoy that red traffic light. She would speak her gratitude list out loud, and in time, she noticed she was much happier—her words of gratitude magnetically bringing more to be thankful for to her life.

I wonder what moment of interruption wants to transform for you to receive your gifts from Source? Perhaps it's the long lineup of shoppers at your supermarket or a half-hour delay at the dentist. Whatever moments have you waiting, write them in the space that follows. As you do, feel them shift into access points of stillness to receive everything that's coming through from the Universe for you.

Watch for Your Windfall

All right, now that you've balanced your masculine and feminine energies and made peace with waiting, you're ready to receive! The Universe has already responded energetically to all that you're asking for. On Earth, however, where matter holds denser energy coupled with our linear perception of time, things can appear to have a lag in showing up.

Knowing this, you can relax if you don't receive something immediately in response to your asking—still, don't be surprised if you do! The Universe works in wondrous ways and with exquisite timing in delivering unique solutions, messages, and teachings to us. It amazes me when I consider the many ways we can Receive from Source. Being open to catch these gifts from the Universe is when life begins to get really colorful for us!

A few of these Divine responses to our questions include:

- Incoming messages delivered in myriad ways, such as signs, books, movies, music, podcasts, conversations, license plates, numbers, billboards, and T-shirt messages.

- People leaving, entering, or reentering your life, either physically, through a phone call, or through text messaging to provide you helpful information and/or support.

- Dreams, synchronous events, and/or mystical experiences connected directly to your challenge.

- A heightening of your clair senses—your psychic sensitivity which corresponds to your senses of seeing, hearing, touching, tasting, and smelling and knowing.

- Sudden unforeseen changes that reorder your life in big and small ways.

Perhaps, in reading this list, you already recognize some of the unique ways your gifts from the Divine are coming to you. Take a moment now to pause and reflect as you mark this page and close your eyes for a moment to review what's already come through anew from the challenge you're working with. Breathe into your heart and notice what information and insights you receive. Perhaps a conversation or maybe a recent dream—recognize these are special gifts for you!

What about the Heavy Stuff?

Do you think nothing can come through your challenge because it seems far too heavy for any of these steps to hold? While that thought can seem true for you, realize it is just a thought, and if you keep it active, then you will be blocked from receiving what is streaming to you from Source.

Take heart, breathe deep, and know that you can create a new thought right now. If you think that the Divine loves you and desires to dovetail with you right now, in the midst of your heaviness and pain, then that is what will open up for you. The heavier your challenge is, the more miracles and potentials are hidden within. This was the case for "Wellness Warrior" Kris Carr.

Kris was diagnosed with a rare, incurable, and inoperable stage IV cancer called epithelioid heman-gioendothelioma (EHE). On the day of her diagnosis, Kris wrote in her journal, "Happy Valentine's Day. You have cancer," which speaks of her black humor and warrior strength in her life's heaviest moment.

At that time, Kris was a young actress and photographer who was burning the candle at both ends. Feeling unwell during a yoga class, she went to a doctor and got the shocking news of the slow-growing vascular cancer that had formed twenty-four undetected tumors in her liver and lungs.

Choosing not to sit very long in the pain of wondering, *How can this be happening to me?*, Kris quickly became the self-appointed "CEO of her well-being" and began interviewing doctors and healers, documenting everything in film, while ruthlessly choosing who and what would be part of her whole health journey to become the "cancer thriver" she is today.

Not only did Kris turn her healing journey into a documentary called *Crazy Sexy Cancer*, she has also written several wellness books as she continues to live a vibrant and inspirational life. "I'm not saying cancer is sexy... What I'm saying is that we are still empowered. We are still alive and whole." Kris Carr's powerful choice to believe in and receive Life's unseen gifts in her heaviest moment transformed her life while empowering countless people in many ways.

As you take all of this in, you might be wondering what you need to do next. It's simple, really; as mentioned before, it's less about *doing* and more about *being.* Be inward focused, be still, be grateful, and be receptive to the many creative ways the Divine aligns with you to give you exactly what you need in the right moment.

If you can move with the intention to receive with an open heart, then your loving gifts will come directly to you, wrapped up in the unique challenge that you're choosing to apply your Creative Intelligence to as you upcycle it. Talk about a masterpiece in process!

Just as we celebrated at the opening of this chapter, I invite you once again to set your book down for a moment to stand and celebrate your transformational journey! This time, when you wrap yourself in that big warm hug, I invite you to breathe everything in because Source is streaming goodness to you all the time, and now that you're open to receive it, life gets really fun!

Celebrate where you have been and where you are now as you step into another Creative Spark to ignite and integrate your receptive powers!

Refresh and Review

- While receiving the gifts that the Divine is abundantly sending your way sounds amazing, it can be challenging to let them in, as it involves being vulnerable and open.

- Your yin/yang energy is directly related to your ability to receive and give. Both energies are different expressions of the same life force energy, which you can observe and balance within.

- Allow for stillness in your life in any form, including moments where you are "stuck" waiting. Come to see such moments as portals for gratitude and receptivity.

- Life has creative methods of sending you solutions, messages, and guidance for your challenges. As you open your heart and awareness, you can receive a windfall from the Universe.

Creative Spark - Step 3

Receive from It
Creative Intelligence Download

- In the quiet of your creative space, place your "Creating in the Unified Field" drawing from the previous chapter's Creative Spark in front of you. Keep a pen and notebook or paper nearby. Reread the three statements at the top of the page; then, gaze again at your spontaneous drawing made in the Unified Field.

- With one hand on your heart and the other on your paper, breathe deeply for five seconds, imagining energy flowing powerfully into your heart center. Hold your breath for five seconds, then exhale for eight seconds. Repeat this process several times while calling to your experience a light feeling or emotion such as joy or appreciation; then bring your challenge to your mind.

- Gently open your eyes and with one hand still connected to your heart, ask again about your challenge: "What might I discover through this?" and "What if you were ultimately a gift?"

- Pick up your pen and begin to automatically write any responses that come through onto your paper. Let your pen move and spill out any words in any way they come—fast/slow, phrases/lists, random/organized—as you keep your focus on your heart while receiving the words without judgment or analysis.

- Trust the Universal Life Force moving through you as the questions activate a response. Don't rush or minimize this step of receiving information from the field. Enjoy calming and energizing your system with your breath while accessing new possibilities. When you feel complete, set your pen down and take a moment to read the words that came through.

- Next, squint your eyes and revisit all the words on your paper. Notice which words seem to jump out at you. Circle the top five words and write them on a new sheet of paper. Feel free to draw around these five special words for you as you doodle, loop, and decorate them. They are important and hold information for your next steps.

Keep in gratitude, the highest form of receiving, and trust that your five special words will bridge into your daily life to reveal more gifts to you. I'll be waiting for you in the next chapter, where you will learn how to act on the information that you received here.

**Imagine this taking place for you now—
See it, feel it, be it!**

Chapter 8

Act on It:
Your Fourth Step to Creating a
Life in Full Colors

Are you ready to learn more for a Life in Full Colors? All the inner work you have done around your challenge up to this point has brought you here to this step: "Act on It." Oh yes! It's now time to take action in response to the Divine's nudges you've been receiving. This action, which has authentic power in it, comes from your powerful alignment with Creator, which you continue to build experientially with each Creative Spark.

Now it's time to uncover how the Divine can propel you to Act on your challenge, transforming it into your superpower. This is a remarkable step! It takes you right out of your default mode into a new trajectory! No more banging around blindly and reliving your unconscious patterns indefinitely. Now you will learn how to sense what your Higher Power is inviting you to do.

In addition to this clarity, you will also learn to recognize your unique helpers who come to support you along the way. This fourth step brings everything you've been transforming inwardly out into the light of day! I can think of no better person to illustrate this step than the first person I met when I moved to Dubai: Theresa Du Toit.

Theresa Transforms Loss

The first time I saw Theresa was at the Mall of the Emirates, when our separate escalators—one going up and one down—met at midpoint.

I remember how we both looked eye to eye and smiled as I silently thought, *That's someone I'd like to spend time with! She dresses more colorfully than I do!* Feeling sleepy with jet lag, I strolled through the seemingly endless mall, growing hungry and tired. Before long, I decided to tuck into a quiet cafe.

You can imagine my surprise when the waitress sat me at a table next to Theresa, who, at this point, was still "the lady on the escalator" to me. As I ate my spinach and feta omelet, Theresa was soon joined by two other women, one with a laptop and all of them in a celebratory mood. Together, over coffee and breakfast, the women guided Theresa through her brand-new website.

Though I didn't know Theresa beyond an escalator smile at that point, it felt so wonderful to take in such a happy scene. Before I left the restaurant that day, I followed an impulse to go over and introduce myself, and that's when she welcomed me to Dubai and invited me for coffee the following week.

When we met again, Theresa shared her story of what she had gone through before that special day in the cafe. I was very touched by what she taught me as she shared her personal challenges with loss. More than a decade earlier, Theresa had arrived in Dubai to start a whole new life for herself. Her husband, Phillip, of thirty years had passed away from cancer rather quickly and unexpectedly, which is why Theresa was starting anew.

In Dubai, she met a warmhearted man named Nick, and they fell deeply in love. Theresa found herself happily married again. However, after only two years of marriage, this loving partnership would also come to an abrupt end. Nick, after a morning of quad biking in the desert, died suddenly of a heart attack. Theresa was brokenhearted and mourned for what felt like ages. She describes this time as "pajama days at home crying buckets and buckets."

During that time of grieving, Theresa also felt something growing within her, "like a pregnant woman." She didn't know what it was exactly or how to make sense of it, but she longed for some way to express it and asked her Higher Power for help.

With a lifelong connection to God, Theresa trusted that her tragedy would bear fruit somehow. In everything, especially the lowest times, she took comfort in these words in the Bible: "I know the plans I have for you, plans to prosper you and not to harm you, plans to give you hope and a future." As Theresa puts it, "Even when life sucks, He can bring our gifts out of us!"

One day, her daughter's friend, a wedding photographer, called Theresa, saying, "I have a business proposition for you! I think you'd be a fabulous wedding celebrant because you're passionate about marriage and you love public speaking!"

Theresa, coming from South Africa, where church weddings were the norm, wondered, *What the heck is a wedding celebrant?* Once she caught on to the possibility, she immediately knew that a career as a wedding celebrant was for her!

Instantly, she sprang into action and began researching all things related to wedding celebrants online. Everything about the career resonated with her, and her action plan grew as she got clarity around how to market herself uniquely. Looking at the myriad websites, Theresa noticed that they all lacked the one thing Theresa was filled with and was ready to express into the world again—a passion for life!

Prior to her grieving period for Nick, Theresa had a clear knowing of her passion: "Life is meant to be celebrated! We are meant to flourish!" It's no surprise that she aligned effortlessly with a career that shares her passion naturally—coaching, inspiring, mentoring, and marrying countless couples intent on joining in vows of love to celebrate building a life together. We all can receive clarity directly from our personal Higher Power on what action we're meant to take. Ready to learn how?

From Pain to Passion

While Theresa's story is unique, the essence of her story is the essence of yours as well. If there's anything that keeps coming through as we move through this book, I hope it's the understanding that your pain-filled challenge is the pivot point to uncovering what lights you up and brings your true colors through!

It could be a new career, a brilliant idea for your well-being, a decision to rebuild a broken relationship—anything! Just like Theresa felt she was "pregnant" but didn't have a clue with her Thinking Mind what it might be, the moment she heard "wedding celebrant," she burst forward into action because, as she says, "It *felt* exactly me."

Learn to trust those periods of life where, on the surface, nothing looks to be happening while underneath there's stirrings of something new being formed. In winter, deep below the ice, waiting for the thaw of spring, new shoots of life are tucked in there, ready to burst through. Each of us holds new shoots we can't yet see.

Sense your hidden potentials within by noticing what lights you up and gives you goose bumps. When your hairs stand on end, that's a signal from your Creative Intelligence! It might feel unclear at first, which is fine; you won't need to sort out it out all by yourself. Most of all, don't lose heart or try to force things to happen; when the time is right, it will become crystal clear what you are meant to do with the stirrings within you.

When we are attuned with Life, we can trust that there is a season for everything to come and go. Nature reminds us that our mourning will turn to laughter and that all of life is changeful. Let that truth comfort you if you feel you have been "pregnant" with something growing within you for some time now. Things are always happening beyond what the eye can see, and Divine Timing will ensure that when it's time to act, all will be aligned and flow easily.

Protect Your Precious Seedling

Remember how Theresa sprang into action immediately upon hearing the words "wedding celebrant"? How she suddenly hopped out of her pajamas and got online to research and learn all she could? Nobody had to tell her to do that. No one had to instruct her about which sites to visit. She just knew! She had a precious seed of an idea, and it was time to Act on It and follow through.

Recognize when this happens to you and seek solitude at such times. Too often, in pure excitement at the freshness of a new idea, we share prematurely and end up being stopped before taking our first precious step forward. Please, keep your new idea very close to you initially, like a precious sprout in a wee cup. Let it grow awhile on its own until it's strong enough and can stand up to the elements outside without being toppled over.

Often the harshest elements to watch for are the voices of those who prefer to keep you from stepping into something new. Even in your unhappiness, there will be some who don't support you taking a new direction, as it disrupts their patterns, which serve them and not you. At times, there are jealous voices who wish they had your amazing idea and may try to stop you so you can't have what they want. Some may even try to take your idea for themselves.

Unfortunately, the strongest resistance usually comes from those closest to you—well-meaning friends and family members—projecting their own stuckness and fear of failure upon you. Consider their perspective as they suddenly see you birth a new idea out of a place that once looked barren. They might be wondering what in the world is happening to you!

This is when the wisdom of retreating into your Creative Space, both your outer and inner one, will serve you well. Anytime you Ask and Receive from the Universe and then get the Divine Impulse to Act on the new information is a time to keep quiet and enjoy tending to the newness. It will grow and be ready to be shared soon enough and, even then, only with trusted ones.

Take a moment now and reflect on those times when something new was struggling to be born in you—an idea, a dream, a vision—and you shared it excitedly to naysayers who shut you down. Review your whole life story and notice what comes to your awareness. Write, doodle, or draw symbols to represent these heavy moments that come up for you in the space provided below. Let them flow right out of your life and onto the page.

Be gentle with yourself here, as you didn't know back then not to overshare your new ideas before they took root. This creative exercise of letting the past go will let you begin again with more awareness.

Now, drawing upon the wisdom you gained from those painful experiences, breathe into your heart and invite all your Creative Intelligence to join you as you write a promise to yourself to protect all your precious seeds of inspiration until they're strong and ready to be shared.

Sunflower Wisdom

So how do you know when to share and with whom? Again, we can look to nature here to help make this clear so that you can stay true to the powerful promise you just made to yourself.

Close your eyes for a moment and imagine a sunflower. Bold and bright, we might assume these sturdy plants rarely move. In truth, these yellow beauties set their gorgeous faces to the sun rising in the east and turn all day to catch it setting in the west. This phenomenon is called heliotropism, and it's seen mostly in young sunflowers before they fully bloom.

Just like sunflowers, we also can sense into light-filled sources of support. Ever notice those bright and radiant people that naturally draw you to them? It's to those ones that you will now turn towards as your challenge continues to transform to the point where you may need a helping hand.

Life will bring you helpers. Some will show up for a little while, and others may walk each step of the way with you to the end; each plays a part in supporting the new potential that is coming through you. Perhaps they have a skill set that will help you move forward, or maybe they provide the emotional support for you to show up in new ways. One thing is clear: you will feel when you need their assistance. Remember, you can ask your Higher Power for the helpers you need, and once requested, know it is done. Expect them to appear!

This very thing happened in Theresa's journey as her grieving subsided and her role as a wedding celebrant was born. When I met her that day in the cafe, she was with her first helpers on her wedding celebrant journey; talented and generous friends who built her a stunning new website. When I asked her later about her impulse to build a site straightaway, she told me, "I knew I needed one after looking at what others were doing online. Once I knew that, people who could help me showed up at the right time with their gifts. God always brings the right people to help us along the way."

Know that your helpers will show up as you expect them to in ways that surprise you. Little did I know—that day I met Theresa with her helpers—the reciprocal role she would play as my own helper in sharing her story so generously for us all to now receive. Trust the process and know that as your challenge transforms into something completely new, so will your awareness of who you can turn to along the way.

Remember, you won't know how it will happen or see every step along your way; you'll only see the one or two you need today. If the Divine showed you everything coming up next for you, you might not believe or feel worthy to receive it all. Things do get better and lighter as you upcycle your challenges this way. We are all meant for an abundant and beautiful journey, and when we cocreate it with Source, changes do come through in light and colorful ways.

From Heavy Hopes to Huge Payoff

Actor Jim Carrey is a great example of not seeing every step but acting (no pun intended) on a strong impulse anyway. Jim grew up poor and dropped out of school as a teenager to work and help with the family bills while developing his comedy. Over time, Jim transformed the challenge of living out of a van in his childhood into an early stand-up routine while he was still a teenager.

In his early twenties, still struggling to get by, Jim took action on his dream and relocated to Los Angeles to pursue comedy. Living out of his car and going to auditions, he would take drives up to Mulholland Drive overlooking the city, park his car, and visualize things he desired coming to him. One of these things in his vision was a check for ten million dollars, which he actually wrote out to himself for acting services and postdated three years in the future. Jim kept that check in his wallet as he honed his craft and auditioned for parts.

Having nothing at that time, Jim said that this ritual of driving and envisioning made him feel better because he knew everything he wanted was "out there"; he simply didn't have all the things in his hands yet. Then, just before the end of that third year, he received that exact amount of money for his role in the box-office hit *Dumb and Dumber*. Reflecting upon his huge payoff with his work and vision combined, Jim emphasized, "You can't just visualize it and then, you know, go eat a sandwich."

Jim makes a good point; as you birth the vision that comes through your unique challenge and take action on all the impulses that spark you into motion, you can expect the payoff that is waiting in the Unified Field for you. Expecting an abundant payoff from the Universe is the next step for you. Before we head that way, let's take a look at what you need to do to ensure you align with this "Act on It" step first.

It's essential to recognize that you will rarely feel completely ready to take your first step, which might feel more like a leap of faith into the unknown. Yet, if you want to progress beyond where you have already been, facing a new direction and stepping boldly forward is the only way.

Fear will meet you here, and that is more than all right. Welcome it in, and if it doesn't leave, simply ask yourself, "Which part of me is afraid?" and love and tend to that part. As you give yourself an inner hug, inquire, "Is this fear even real right now?" You'll come to find that it likely isn't and your Thinking Mind is simply overreacting to the newness. Move your focus into your heart and receive all the love and courage that is always available for you there.

Recognize that you are never alone on your journey. Your Creator is with you each step you take. From here you can let go of any last traces of fear. When you take a bold step forward into the unknown, aware of the whole Universe stepping with you, you discover that you dovetail directly into the many miracles that are ever present for you!

Refresh and Review

- Unseen potentials grow within you during your most challenging moments, and your Creative Intelligence prompts you to take action when they are ready to be born.

- Keep your first steps toward a new idea quiet, as there are those who will try to dissuade you from stepping into something new before you even start because they feel safe in your sameness.

- As you progress on your journey, there will always be helpers along the way who can be identified through their radiance and lightness.

- Taking a big step forward into new terrain can feel scary. Have courage and step boldly, knowing you are never alone when you are cocreating with your Creator.

Creative Spark - Step 4

Act on It
Creative Action Step

- In the quiet of your creative space, set a piece of paper in front of you along with your coloring materials.

- Set your most recent Creative Spark, your "Creative Intelligence Download," nearby and read your five special words again that you circled. They hold information to help inform your next steps. Keep them nearby as your "helpers" while you create your next step forward.

- With one hand on your heart and the other on your paper, breathe deeply and slowly, imagining light-filled energy flowing upward from the center of the Earth through your feet, up through your body, and shooting straight out of your head. See that light continue up through the ceiling as it continues up into the blackness of space. Follow it up until you can sense a brilliant white light.

- Imagine a small portal opening to the light and pass through it. Feel yourself dissolve and merge with the brilliant bright light. This is the Creative Source of all of life! See yourself as pure Creative Intelligence energy now. Feel it!

- As Creative Intelligence, in a clear voice, state, "Creator, I command my next action step to be made clear to me. Show me!" Then feel, sense, and notice what is shown to you. Take your time. Sense the information coming through. Know it's there and that it will become even clearer to you as you draw.

- Pick up a crayon and draw a large outline of a footprint onto your paper. Whether it's a barefoot shape with toes or an outline of a shoe doesn't matter. This foot symbolizes the first step you will take.

- Within your footprint shape, begin to write and record whatever thoughts, information, and intelligence you received as you went into your inner Creative Universe. Perhaps you got a nudge to reconnect with an old friend or to take an online course on a topic of interest. Maybe you got a strong sense to get a second opinion on a health issue that is concerning you. Whatever next steps you received, record them within the footprint. Even if your guidance is telling you to wait and not take any action right now, record that.

- Continue to add colors, symbols, shapes, and doodles into the footprint to enhance your next action step. As you do this, welcome any new intuitive hits or hunches that come through to your awareness.

- Next, in the open space surrounding your footprint, begin to list your sources of love and support in your life. The ones who you know will walk beside you as you take this new bold step forward. They might be friends, loved ones, mentors, aspects of nature, spiritual practices, or guides from the spirit realm. You may have others I haven't listed or a combination of these. As you look at all you wrote around your next step, feel all of your supports reflected back to you!

- Finally, find a special place in your drawing to write in bold, colorful letters: "ALL OF LIFE SUPPORTS ME IN MY NEXT STEPS!"

Know you can go up to your Higher Power at any point in time to get more information and clarity as you take more steps forward. I'll be just beyond this page, waiting to share with you all the wonder your newfound sense of expectation can open up for you!

Imagine this taking place for you now—
See it, feel it, be it!

Chapter 9

Expect It:
Your Fifth Step to Creating a Life in Full Colors

All these transformational steps you are learning and taking are creating deep change. You are doing what few choose to do with their challenge. By working with the creative material that the painful pieces of your life provides, you are not only aligned with your Divine Creative Intelligence; you're also deepening your trust in Source support you each step of the way.

You can anticipate this growing inner strength and Divine support to factor into your daily life and bring plenty of magical moments to you. This is the essence of your next step towards creating a Life in Full Colors. When it comes to upcycling your challenge in the way you are learning to do here, you can now "Expect It" to surprise and delight you.

Going forward, we'll look at the joy you can now Expect as you lighten your energy up. In addition, you'll learn how to release any misconceptions that creating a Life in Full Colors means a challenge-free life. From there, we'll explore how you can Expect to soften your judgments. Finally, we'll see how expecting the best from your challenges naturally forms a kinder and more loving version of you. Truly, this is a time of empowered compassion unfolding within you. Hold onto your brushes because things are about to get really vibrant and colorful!

Aloha Spirit in Bangkok

Expecting to be surprised and delighted by your challenge might sound too good to be true. There were many years where I wouldn't have believed it possible myself, so I understand any doubts you might have. What I can offer you is a little story from my life that may help quiet your skepticism.

My family and I moved to Thailand from Japan, and this story is from the early months of settling there. I was still in the uncomfortable stage of being in between two very different worlds. I was no longer living in Japan, but I didn't yet feel as though Bangkok was my home either. I asked the Universe to help lift my heavy heart, and fully expected it to do so.

Because I've lived almost as many years abroad as I have in Canada, my true home sits within my heart. While homesickness doesn't really bother me, during transitions, I have noticed I get a strong pull to see and be with the people and places that lift my spirits while grounding me.

In the early days of transitioning to Thailand, I found myself longing to be with my younger sister Shelley. Family and friends tend to call her "Shell," which sums her up quite well, as she lives on the North Shore of Oahu, Hawaii and can spend hours combing beaches for beautiful little shells. She's a quiet soul who can find beauty in all things, especially in those that are often overlooked.

One weekday morning, as I stepped out of my Thai language class and into the bright sun to walk to the train, I felt the density of the city close in on me. It was Shell's birthday, and when I tried to call her, our different time zones got in the way.

Walking along the disjointed sidewalk, a wave of longing overtook me as I felt the congested city weighing me down. To ground myself, I breathed deep, closed my eyes, and asked Divine for help. Walking on, I imagined my feet bare in the sand and suddenly got the impulse to treat myself to a pedicure. The idea was so strong and energizing that I sensed that Source was Creating Healing and upcycling my heaviness with me.

Bangkok is a city filled with nail spas that provide a cool and quiet mini-retreat. As I carried on walking, I fully expected to find one. Suddenly, I received such a strong impulse to turn down a little street that I just had to follow it.

That's when I saw it. I held my breath for a moment and then slowly smiled to see a brightly painted ALOHA sign hanging in front of me. Marveling at Life's sense of humor, I realized the sign was for a very small nail spa, so I stepped inside. And then...I was in Hawaii!

After a warm welcome of *"Aloha! Sawadee Kha!"* by the two women working inside, I was sat down in a comfortable chair where I stared wide-eyed at shelves overflowing with ukuleles, wood-carved pineapples, and endless shells! Looking up, my eyes took in a sea of multicolored leis hanging from the ceiling. To be cared for with so much *aloha* was more than enough, and yet, the story doesn't end there.

When the stereo began to play music by Oahu's own Jack Johnson, I smiled big and took it as a sign to call Shell again. This time, she answered, and as I described to her where I was and how I got there, she laughed and got me completely, just as I knew she would. After our call ended, I sat recalling all the times the Universe had transformed my heaviness so wondrously this way. Like a stack of evidence, all those moments lined up clearly in my mind.

No wonder the Creative Intelligence in me fully expected to cocreate something new with all my unsettled and ungrounded energy. It had proved its powerful support to me enough times over that I was certain it would do so again. The lift from Source that morning was so specific and aligned that it brought me a much-needed sense of ease and a connection both to the people and places that were a part of my new life in Thailand. It was soon after that magical day that I began to think of and call Bangkok "home."

Expect the Joy to Pile Up

Once we start to learn how to play with Life this way, the number of experiences which we can label "joy-filled" naturally piles up. This joy, by the way, is very different from fleeting moments of happiness, which come and go conditionally. It's more of a knowing joy, embedded into every fiber of our being. This joy is based upon a solid foundation of trust in your Creative Intelligence to cocreate with you in order to transform what may seem to be a mess into a masterpiece.

When we have that level of trust, our "joy data" stacks so high that it's simply expected that the Divine will intervene and lift us up. Now, if you're reading this and thinking, *Maybe that works for you, but not so much for me*, please know, I hear you. Truly, I have felt and spoken those very same words before too. What's required of you is to *use the tools* within these steps I'm sharing so that your own "joy data" piles so high that your expectation grows too.

When I first began using these steps to meet each of my challenges, there was a tipping point when enough data piled up that I knew to Expect Creator to bring me elegant solutions for my joy. Coming to that place of knowing that you can Expect the Universe to lift and support you happens for each of us in our own timing, of course.

Not only will the joy show up for you, but it will be felt by those around you too. Everything that is felt is shared—like the laughter and giggles from the women working at the nail spa as I squeezed my six-foot-one body into a tiny floral muumuu, their Hawaiian version of a spa robe, which hugged me a little too cozily, I might add!

Soften Your Judgments

To consistently experience this natural levity in your life, it's essential to Expect challenges to exist in the world of form. So please, from now on, drop any judgments you have about having challenges show up in your life. Yes, you read that correctly. If there's any part of you that thinks Creating a Life in Full Colors means your life will now be challenge free, you can let that part go completely.

While that seems like such a joy-kill statement, I assure you, it's none of the sort. Our challenges are here by Divine Design! Source laid it all out that way to ensure that the newness our struggles bring through us would continually expand us beyond our limiting stories of who we are. As we alchemize our challenges, they reveal more possibilities to us. Expansive ones we couldn't yet see.

Pause a moment and lay your eyes on all the created forms around you—the window, a pen, a cushion, maybe even a clock. Everything around you was initially imagined and then formed in response to the challenge of living without it for some time. Actually, look right under you. What are you sitting on? Likely a chair or a sofa.

At one point in a chairless world, someone, likely with a very sore back and bottom, grew sick and tired of sitting on a hard, dirty floor. The challenge of living with no seating alternatives sparked their Creative Intelligence to take action to form a chair!

Everything created by humans in our world of form was sparked by a desire for something new to come through. Unless we are consciously cocreating with Source, we are at risk of bringing through objects and situations that are not for the highest good of all.

We are all wired to create, and the best use of our Creative Intelligence is to flow that power into those situations that shake up our lives! You can soften your judgments around having challenges arise by honoring the essential part they play in the process of expansion. So many of us pick up messages along our way that we're bad or have failed if our life isn't challenge free. If you're struggling with such thoughts, let's create a way to release them now. All you need are colored crayons or markers and a few minutes here with me.

Soften into that childlike wonder of yours and direct your breath into your heart space as you choose a color that feels most like the judgments that come up around the word "challenge" to you. Is it a dense gray? A blast of red? Alarming orange?

Just take the first color your eyes look at and write the word "challenge" in the following space. As you drop the each of the letters onto the page, drop all your judgments around living a life with challenges. Color around, in, and through the word "challenge" completely, using any colors you like. Flood the space with color until the word is fully dissolved.

Notice what happens inside of you when you drop and dissolve the word "challenge" into a bath of colors while releasing all of your judgments too.

Now, it's time to Expect more magic as you transform "challenge" into a whole new word. Open your heart and mind up to the possibility of turning "challenge" into "opportunity"!

Go ahead; take a new color that expresses the "opportunity" that a life of growth and infinite possibility holds. Notice how you feel now as you write the word "opportunity" within the next space provided. Surround it with colors that represent brand new opportunities to you, filling the entire space.

How was it to playfully soften any judgments that way? What did you notice within you as your Creative Intelligence came through? Did you feel yourself relax as you playfully transformed words this way? To see "opportunity" sitting right in front of you invites a big dose of curiosity to join into the mix too. You can begin to wonder, *What and who else can I expect to join me?*

The day I relaxed and let the Aloha Spirit envelop me, a whole new opportunity was forming, which I only realized months later. Bangkok's intensity created the space within me to imagine living somewhere with palm trees, white beaches, and clear blue water. Specifically, near a beach with shells!

It wasn't surprising then to me when at the end of our third year in Bangkok, we were moving once again. This time to Dubai. I wondered about the move and what to expect. While known for luxury, modernity, and endless skyscrapers, Dubai gave me something else completely. For my family and me, Dubai offered us a much-longed-for wide blue sky and a spacious home only a three-minute walk from a shell-filled beach.

See Yourself Anew

By softening your judgments about your challenges, something beautiful happens within you. Quite naturally, you become softer and easier on yourself.

Your inner nag also softens and quiets down. You may not have to give your inner nag a new gig from here on in because your growing self-love will assure the most judged pieces of you.

As you step anew into opportunities, there may be moments when that critical voice thinks you're transforming too quickly. Remember, that part of you likes to keep things running the same as always. At such times, that nagging voice may show up in full force and even startle you. Be easy at such moments and even grateful.

Your inner nag is your small, conditioned self and is only trying to protect you, perhaps by reminding you of times in your past that didn't go so well and bear a resemblance where you're heading now. In such charged moments, where your inner nag is in full force, intend to keep in your softness and sit with it. Your inner nag can reveal a wound from long ago that needs to be tended to. Thank it, above all else, and honor how it is revealing heavy pieces that need care and tending to. Another helper for your journey of healing, integrating, and expressing all the colors of who you truly are!

Embrace It All

As we include and honor all the pieces of ourselves that we once avoided, we naturally create healing and become whole. Canadian singer, composer, and nature conservationist Ann Mortifee speaks to this beautifully. Ann starts her days in the quiet of the early morning to meditate and reflect on life. Some years ago, she began to capture her morning musings, much like direct downloads from the Divine.

She set her written reflections down over the course of a year to create a best-selling book entitled *In Love with the Mystery*. Her book is a mystical wonder, which I (along with Oprah Winfrey) highly recommend.

Through Ann's deep connection to nature, she invites us to tend to every piece of ourselves, especially the most tender parts, trusting that even when things feel most bleak, nothing is ever completely lost. She reminds us, "Just when you think the winter will never cease, suddenly spring appears. So it is with sadness, sorrow, loneliness, or loss. A new bud will appear...a new life will be felt among the ruins. Have faith. Expect the impossible. Trust the unfolding nature of life. Wait an eternity if need be. Spring, inevitably, will surely come."

I invite you, from here onward, with an intensity that you have never allowed yourself before, to Expect opportunity-filled challenges to show up for you. Welcome them into your life without self-judgment, shame, or blame. Along with this, if you can "expect the impossible" as Ann invites us to, then the wonder of miracles in all shapes and sizes can be expected too.

How could I have known to trust that Loving Guidance leading me to that little ALOHA sign down a narrow lane I had never before seen? As poet M.C. Richards describes it, "Not knowing and trusting simultaneously." I didn't know how or what gifts the Divine would bring to my unsettled heart, but I trusted life and expected without a doubt that in the right moment, something new and better would appear.

Refresh and Review

- By engaging with these transformational tools while flowing your unlocked Creative Intelligence into your challenges, you deepen your trust both in Life and yourself.

- Once you're in a natural rhythm of playing and cocreating with Source in transforming your challenges, you will see your "joy data" naturally pile up.

- Dissolve any judgments around having challenges in your life by perceiving them as opportunities instead.

- When stepping into new opportunities, your "inner nag" may show up to reveal hidden wounds that need tending to for your continued growth.

- Expect opportunity-filled challenges to show up as an integral part of your creative experience. As you trust the process, you can also Expect miracles to show up too!

Creative Spark - Step 5

Expect It
A Creative Surprise

- In the quiet of your creative space, gather these materials: a set of children's paints, brushes, a jar of water, and eight pieces of paper. Stack and set the paper in front of you along with the paints, brushes, and water. Have your other art materials and a journal with a pen nearby, as you may need them for the latter half of this Creative Spark.

- With one hand on your heart and the other on your paper, breathe deeply and slowly, imagining light-filled energy flowing upward from the center of the Earth through your feet, up through your body, and shooting straight out of your head. See that light continue up through the ceiling into the blackness of space until you can see a brilliant white light.

- Imagine a small portal opening to the light and pass through it. Feel yourself dissolve and merge with the brilliant bright light. This is the Creative Source of all of life! See yourself as pure Creative Intelligence energy now. Feel it!

- Connect with the light of Creator and say, "Creator, surprise and delight me as we cocreate here now. Show me!"

- Open your eyes and then feel, sense, and see what paint color you're most attracted to. Use this one color for the first part of this Creative Spark. Plunge your brush into the water so that the paint can move and slide easily and fill your brush with your special color now.

- Begin to paint circle shapes (see the full list below) on a fresh piece of paper for a minute or two. Paint circles only until you are painting shapes on top of shapes with no more space left. At that point, slide the circle painting out of the way, take a fresh piece of paper, and move to the next shape on the list and paint it in the same color, filling the paper.

  - Circles
  - Squares
  - Zigzags
  - Triangles

- Moons
- Dots
- Spirals

- Continue this way down the whole list, one by one, each new shape on a new piece of paper with the same color until you have seven different papers filled with seven different shapes.

- Once all seven of your papers are completely filled, gather them all together and take a look at your Creative Intelligence reflecting back at you from each page.

- Now, rip each of the shape-filled, painted papers up into several tiny pieces. Yes, you read that right! Even if you don't want to, tear each page apart into little bits. Really get into the motion of ripping and as you do, release any resistance in you.

- Now, make a pile of the torn pieces and take a moment to breathe and connect into your heart as you set the intention to create anew. Notice what impulse comes to you. Maybe you feel pulled to use all the pieces to form a sort of mosaic, gluing each piece onto a new paper, then drawing and painting into it. Or perhaps you get the desire to fold, twist, glue, and paint the pieces into a sculptural form. Whatever you do, ensure you include at least one torn piece of paper into the new creation that comes through you.

- Remain curious and play with what attracts you and, above all, be easy with yourself. Something always shows up when you create from a relaxed state.

- Go up to your Higher Power at any point to get loving guidance and support if you need. Once you feel complete, write down your feelings about the experience in a journal if desired and set your surprise creation somewhere special where it can remind you that Source truly loves to surprise and delight you in many ways! Expect it!

I'll meet you in the next chapter where we'll look at how you can feel and experience more of this unending love from the Universe each and every day.

**Imagine this taking place for you now—
See it, feel it, be it!**

Chapter 10

Love It:
Your Sixth Step to Creating a
Life in Full Colors

Ill right, dear one, it is time to move into a step I truly love to share. I think you will love it too. Love and harmony form naturally in you when your need to engage with disharmony is through. This step is inviting you to see your challenges through the eyes of love. As you choose to "Love It," watch this love transform you!

That's why there is no space here for the disharmony that comes with shame or regret. Knowing our challenges are opportunities for growth and transformation, they can be met in real time with love and respect. With each of these steps you're learning, your past challenges are transforming into your present wisdom. Once you create healing with a challenge, there's no need to walk through it again. As you Love and integrate it, both the heavy emotions and the light, things naturally come into a balance and harmony for you.

There is no higher love than this. Outmoded concepts such as "getting it perfect" simply drop away in this love. You come to see that you can have any conditions arise and Love them all with the knowledge that they will ultimately support your growth and expansion.

Up ahead, we'll examine the power of unconditional love and explore what that level of love truly
is and what it can open up in you. Building upon
this, we'll look at what a love-empowered intention
can do for you and all those in your field of energy.
You'll complete this love-filled learning by discovering playful ways to disrupt your same old patterns
while embracing the spontaneity that ensues.

Seeing beyond the Surface

Opening up to unconditional love deepens our
experience of it phenomenally. Wherever you are
and whatever situation you encounter in your life,
you can always choose to see and sense Divine love
within it, far beyond what is visible in the material
world. This is especially helpful when your challenge
is ongoing and seemingly bleak with no clear end
in sight.

Moving from Bangkok to Dubai reinforced this in
my life journey. When it came time to move again,
we set out together as a family, knowing transitions always include "bumps in the road," as new
challenges surface to help us grow. Sure enough,
our challenge showed up, not as a "bump in the
road" but more like a "wave in the sea."

Shortly after the container that held all of our household possessions set sail, the shipping company fell bankrupt. That meant no port would allow the ship with our container entry. With no clear sign as to when we would see our things again, I chose to set my frustrations and concerns that arose within me straight into these seven steps. As I owned, asked, received, and acted upon answers from my Source, I rediscovered a deep peace within me. I expected that calming from Source.

Living for those first months in Dubai without the bulk of our material possessions made it clear just how little we needed. With a roof over our heads and a few pots, dishes, and beds, we still had more than many in the world do, sadly. With all the intensity in those first months of adjusting to a new city—new schools, new roads, new rules, new systems, new culture—a near-empty home held us in peaceful simplicity. Remembering how the density of Bangkok engulfed and at times overwhelmed us, this ship out at sea began to feel like a special moving-in gift from the Divine.

Finally, after several months, our container could dock and was delivered to us. The funny thing is, when it all arrived, there were so many things we didn't even need. I learned a lot as I came to Love and be grateful for this challenge. It allowed so many fearful pieces of me to be revealed, healed, and integrated.

More than this, I felt held and loved by Source while I moved through each step to pivot my heaviness for the light. This is a love that is like no other. A love that is accepting, wise, and aware that every situation can help us grow. This love is available to us all the time because it is who we truly are. The problem is all the stuff we have around us that we deem important can cover this love up. To experience this Divine love within all the waves that rise up in our lives is what we will now explore.

Loving Unconditionally

Let's begin by looking at what unconditional love is. For many of us, unconditional love means loving others no matter what. Actually, this loving "others" part is quite the opposite of what it means. The one condition we all share in the world we live in is that we live in a world of projections. Each of us is a projection of the Universal Intelligence experiencing itself in form. While a projection standing in front of you appears as another, in the shape of your friend, or your child, or the waitress taking your order, in actuality, each one is you experiencing life from another perspective.

To be clear, the love we are talking about when we explore unconditional love is not the "I love horses" or "I love spicy food" kind of love. The love we are looking at is the eternal wave of time and space emanating from Source. Unconditional love then is the act of loving yourself in each and every time and space projection that shows up in front of you. This is the highest love there is, and it begins within each of us. Only by having this understanding and acceptance for every projection that appears to reveal unacknowledged parts of you can you experience love unconditionally.

With this upgraded definition of unconditional love, you can now understand how essential creating a Life of Full Colors is for you and why you were pulled to learn these steps. Your Creative Intelligence guides you to what your soul needs most in each stage of its journey. Each of us is being guided on our soul's journey to merge into this Divine love. Well done for staying the course. As you Love your challenges and leverage them for your transformation, it benefits everybody in your energy field and beyond.

If I had stayed stuck in my knee-jerk reactivity toward our shipping company, othering and blaming them for my frustration born from my small fears around potentially losing our household things, I would have missed out on a huge opportunity. By asking Source what I could learn while looking for the gift within, I was able to uncover and Love the unacknowledged parts of myself, which I had kept out at sea away from me. It was only when I decided to soften my outer gaze and turned inwardly to heal my heavy emotions that my heart opened to consider the those connected to the shipping company, specifically to the men working on that ship.

I heard news of the crew who were also stuck out at sea with our container. They were living in far worse conditions than I have ever known in my lifetime. Floating aimlessly with no clarity about their jobs, no contact with their families back home, and no idea what their fate might be, these were clearly unacknowledged pieces of me asking to be recognized and loved. I was humbled and moved to pray for the crew, asking the Divine how I might help them or anyone around me in need. The more I focused my energy, the more insight I received, and the biggest lesson was that "them" actually meant "me."

I began talking to people in my neighborhood and learned of many in need locally in Dubai. While I had no way of helping the boat crew directly, it turned out that there were many organizations supporting individuals in need to whom I could volunteer my help and time and resources. There were also families in my community who needed and appreciated the extra bikes, bedding, furniture, and other household items from our container when it finally arrived a few months later.

Through it all I met many warmhearted people from around our globe who had also come to live in Dubai. People caring deeply for their personal and their global family and doing their best to provide a life of health, happiness, and love. All of us, giving and receiving together alike.

Love in Unity and Responsibility

Awareness of our unity is essential as we grow in Universal Love. Each one of us holds the potential to create healing for ourselves and those in our Earth family. You, Dear Creator, are beautifully awake to creative power. At the same time, many are still on their journeys to uncover theirs. Regardless of where we are in our journeys, we are all formed with this Universal Creative Intelligence that can upcycle heaviness into light. When we remember this and honor our shared roots from the one Source, our combined colorful expression only grows and strengthens our unity.

Our inner work has a strong effect on those around us, which means we have a responsibility to ensure we maintain our intention for unconditional love and oneness. We have great power when we focus our energy to transform whatever shows up before us into wisdom. As you continue to choose this less-traveled way, you will encounter many who won't understand or appreciate the love-filled work you are doing. Don't let this deter you. Keep on, step-by-step, and know your helpers will always appear and that you are never alone.

Remember, this is not the way most people choose to live their lives. Most need to have something happen materially in order to say, "I love my life!" You now know that nothing needs to happen outwardly when you are filled up from within and cocreating with Source.

Perhaps before reading this book, you may have felt stuck in that place of "waiting to fall in love with life" once your challenge faded away. Of course, such waiting is futile, as all challenges require our responsiveness and intentional engagement. Each moment that we take responsibility and act in love allows the Divine to shine radiantly through our broken pieces and light our way forward.

Creating a Life You Love Each Day

We can choose love right now without setting conditions for an imagined future. I think of those I have met who have had near-brushes with death and now fully appreciate the minutiae of life and wonders so often overlooked. Like the mouth-watering aroma bubbling from a pot or the soft rustling of the wind through the trees, seemingly common moments such as these hold immense love.

The question is, are you living your moments expecting to be surprised and met by love, or are you set on default mode? Take stock of all the things you do in the same way every day. Imagine a typical day in your mind and note all the routines that you run through. Go ahead. Close your eyes and think about these routines.

It can be surprising to really stop, look, and see all the patterns running in our daily routines. Here's another little surprise for you; nobody is forcing you to hold to your repetitive modes of operating. You can create new ways of being and disrupt any patterns needing to be upgraded and infused with your intention for joy and love. You can choose to create each day in a colorful new way!

Maybe you start your day anew by greeting the morning sun with a barefoot stroll on your lawn. You might switch to your nondominant hand while brushing your hair and teeth, giving your brain a fun workout while you break routine. Try asking (rather than ignoring) your body's wisdom as you inquire what it would like to wear, eat, and how it wants to pace the day. As you do this and listen closely, you will find that some days call for bold color, intense flavor, and bursts of activity while others call for soft color, subtle simplicity, and complete calm. However you are inspired, as you create each day, you can be sure that your spontaneity will expand your experience and love for life.

Use this space to write out all the ways you desire to create more spontaneity in your day; from the moment you pop your eyes open to the moment they shut. As you write and invite newness into your life, be forewarned as more magic and fun will show up for you! Each pattern you let go of opens up space for your loving Source to delight and surprise you.

The Next Thing Is Love

This act of letting go for the new to come through reminds me of those who have left a job, relationship, or situation they didn't feel aligned with and come for a Creating Healing session, holding the question, "What's next?" For most people, tucked within their question is a strong desire to create a more meaningful experience.

I've noticed a similar response comes through for each intentional "What's next?" question when their

Creative Intelligence surfaces and flows into the artwork. The Universal theme being, "Before you do anything new, take some time to love, nurture, and tend to for yourself right now. You are very special and worthy of all the love that you long to give to others."

Meaningless busyness will only bring another cycle of unhappiness; the moment we truly realize this Divine Guidance is pure gold. Self-love is the foundation from where meaningful next steps come. This act of slowing down to fill ourselves up beyond full with love is what bursts our old pattern of over-giving from emptiness completely apart. As we choose self-love consistently, we overflow with meaning and purpose, fully powered by Source paving our way forward.

Without a doubt, Source will empower all your loving intentions so that your "next thing," whether in work, love, or anything else, will arise naturally to your awareness with a clarity for your next steps.

However, if you don't shift your outward focus to turn your gaze inwardly and strengthen your loving connection with your Higher Power—which is your innermost Authentic Self—then your challenges will pull you down rather than elevate and expand you. Most of all, you will miss out on the wondrous experience of yourself as the love that you truly are.

Remember that Life has got you; it will never let you go. You can see it through the people who suddenly show up in your life, through the situations that open up, and through the many precious moments that reflect the constant love tucked within all your challenges back to you. When you come to know them to be reflections of the countless versions of yourself, you can't help but love them all!

If you choose to perceive through the eyes of love, then you will naturally emanate that same unconditional love flowing to you, 24-7. Once you know yourself as this love, aware of itself dressed up in a human disguise, you have come home to yourself. Such a homecoming is felt and enjoyed by everyone around you. In fact, your next and final step to a Life in Full Colors is to share your love and wisdom outwardly. This is true love at its best: expansive and free, inside and out.

Refresh and Review

- Knowing your creative power to transform situations, you can be in any circumstance and choose Love.

- As you choose to see and Love the part of yourself reflected back to you in every person who shows up in your life, you learn to Love unconditionally.

- We hold a great responsibility to focus our awareness of how to upcycle whatever challenge shows up before us for the highest good for all.

- We're all given twenty-four precious hours each day within which we can intentionally create new and loving ways.

Creative Spark - Step 6

Love It
Create a Blast of Unconditional Love

- In the quiet of your creative space, gather your crayons, paints, brushes, a tub of water, and a large piece of paper (or two smaller pieces taped together).

- With one hand on your heart and the other on your paper, breathe deeply and slowly, imagining light-filled energy flowing upward from the center of the Earth through your feet, up through your body, and shooting straight out of your head. See that light continue up through the ceiling into the blackness of space until you can see a brilliant white light.

- Imagine a small portal opening to the light and pass through it. Feel yourself dissolve and merge with the brilliant bright light. This is the Creative

Source of all of life! See yourself as pure Creative Intelligence energy now. Feel it!

- Connect with the light of the Creator and say, "Creator of all that is, I command you to create a blast of unconditional love for the highest good of all as we cocreate here and now. Show me!"

- Open your eyes and then sense what color you're most attracted to. Use this color to either paint or draw a circle the size of your closed fist in the middle of your paper.

- Next, inside the circle, draw two triangles, overlapping, one on top of the other, with the first one pointing upward and the second one pointing downward to form a six-pointed star within your circle.

- Draw a shape or symbol representing your unconditional loving Authentic Self into the center of the star. As you draw and color it in, reflect upon the six steps that you have learned so far—"Own It," "Ask on It," "Receive from It," "Act on It," "Expect It," and "Love It."

- Paint six lines that radiate out from each of the six points of the star. Paint them to the far edge of your paper. While you are painting these six lines, consider how each of the six steps that you learned and experienced in your art and life have helped to transform your challenge into wisdom and lighter colored emotions.

● Begin to paint into this radiant star with the colors that seem to call out to you. Step by step and point by point, fill your paper with the colors that light you up and express your radiant, colorful love.

● Take your time and enjoy all the feelings that flow through you as you ply your unique colors into, through, and all around your star. See its beams of love and light blasting out for all to receive as you live a Life in Full Colors; a pure expression of the radiant love that you are.

● If there are any words that come to your awareness as you paint, feel free to include them in this beautiful blast of unconditional love. Continue painting until you feel complete and take time to look upon your star's radiance so that you receive all the love it's flowing out to you.

I'll meet you in the next chapter, your final step, where we'll look at how this blast of love from the Universe is shared far beyond the edges of who we think ourselves to be!

**Imagine this taking place for you now—
See it, feel it, be it!**

Chapter 11

Share It:
Your Seventh Step to Creating a Life in Full Colors

Here we are, at the seventh and final step of Creating a Life in Full Colors: "Share It." It's my wish that what you have learned has brought you into a more loving relationship with yourself. Your healing journey here has almost come full circle. And now this circle needs to be closed so that it can be completed for you. By sharing your wisdom and experiences, you close your circle while naturally opening new ones up for others to share with you.

When we think about sharing, it's easy to misunderstand what this means. We've all had the experience of being at the mercy of someone pouring out a steady stream of "let me tell you all about it" advice without considering if we really want to hear it. Rarely is this sort of sharing impactful or appreciated. I know, as I have played both parts such conversations, unfortunately.

I notice, however, as I quiet into the Source within me, I relax and move in my loving power, and any forced sharing stops.

In the coming chapter you will learn how your personal inner changes and shifts in perspective get shared organically. Next, we will look at how you can Share your loving perspective, either silently or with words from the heart. Finally, you will explore the profound interconnectedness between the collective human heart and the heart of our planet. The phrase

"We are One" will hold a deeper meaning for you from this point on.

A Taxi Ride to Remember

The first time I experienced sharing these seven healing steps from the silent space of my heart was in a taxi ride after a red-eye flight many years ago. As you can imagine, after an overnight flight, I dropped into the back seat, tired and hoping for a little nap. But my driver, a quiet gray-haired Vietnamese man, welcomed me with a warm smile, so I smiled back at him, and after a minute or two, we got to making small talk about travel, which led to us talking about Vietnam. When I told him how much I loved traveling and eating the scrumptious street food in his home country, it was like a switch flipped.

Suddenly, my shy driver opened up his heart and began to share his complicated life story with me as we sped down the freeway. While he spoke of the many challenges he was experiencing, I thought of each of the seven steps and the Creative Intelligence within us all. I embraced the inner knowing that his struggles held infinite potentials. Rather than feel sorry for him, or try to help or fix him, I held it all in its wonderful chaos, knowing how truly blessed he was.

All the struggles and messes are integral parts of our ever-unfolding journey back home to our Source within. While sitting in silence with an open heart as he opened up to me was all I could do as a passenger in that cab, I sensed that being present with his story in the awareness that the potential is there for him to step into the place of "owning it" was more than enough.

As he dropped me off, he turned to me in the back seat and thanked me. He told me I was the kindest lady he ever talked with in his cab. I was touched but also surprised. I had simply said, "Hello," told him my destination, and mentioned how I enjoyed traveling and eating my way through Vietnam. But I knew what he meant. It wasn't about the words; it was about my perspective of him. He was energetically experiencing the loving energy with which I held him and his potential-filled story as I listened.

Being Present

It's a funny thing we tend to do as humans. We appreciate the intrinsic beauty in a tree or a sunset that we gaze upon, yet with other human beings we can often overlook the innate beauty within. Each of us longs to be seen and acknowledged for the essence of who we are. We can give the person standing in front of us the same appreciation as we do the sky and trees.

Being present with another is exactly this. In fact, seeing another's Divine nature and infinite potential is exactly how Source views us all the time. You can't help but have an impact on someone when you choose to see them through the loving eyes of Source.

You may be wondering, *How on earth can I aspire to see another person through the same higher perspective as Source!? I'm a human being and that's a big reach!* I know, it sounds impossible, and actually, *it is* when you're seeing through the eyes of your small, reactive, conditioned self. Yet when you look and see as the Creative Intelligence you are, fully aware of the underlying beauty in all the messy and painfilled challenges of life, you can make that loving reach!

More Ways to Share It

Be the one who, in full compassion, knows that heart-break can open a door to healing and change. Be the one who understands that pain has the potential to peel away masks while dissolving disconnection from Source. Be the one who sees that our struggles can open us up to new levels of vulnerability, honesty, trust, and resilience, especially when everything falls apart.

Share your wealth of wisdom by listening as the Divine healer you are, and those in your presence will feel your energetic embrace to one day activate the Divine healer within themselves. Listen to your strong inner voice, and, if useful, words will spontaneously come through you. A Source-inspired impulse to speak is yet another way to Share with another.

How do you know your smaller self isn't speaking up to rescue or fix the things that need to break down for new growth to come through? Keep your focus in your heart as you observe yourself. Sense in and feel if you are breathing deeply and slowly. Notice if you are present without being triggered by their story. Observe if you can listen intently while keeping a calm spaciousness within you. If you can, then you are centered in Source.

Should there be any vital words to say, they will come through you without being scripted or forced in any way in order to support shifting another's heaviness into light. Stay open and true, and, if needed, wise words from Source will flow through you. Above all, if nothing moves your heart to speak, trust this and keep in your silent presence, listening closely from your heart.

Two Hearts Attuned

Our planet is also a living being with a heart, and like the micro to the macro, the human heart is profoundly interconnected with the Earth's heart. Our planet's electromagnetic field quite literally pulls us into her, as a mother holds her child to her breast.

Recent science reveals that there is an energetic reciprocity between human beings and our planet that is one and the same. We have the power to impact the Earth's magnetic field. Our collective connection to Earth and to one another in shared electromagnetic frequencies means we are an interconnected family of shared energy.

This interconnectedness was made visible during the tragic events in New York on the morning of September 11, 2001, when people's individual and collective thoughts and feelings fed directly into our planet's electromagnetic field. Researcher Greg Braden shares this story and its significant impact on science as well as our human history.

There are two satellites that measure the electromagnetic field of our planet. These reflect the activity of the Earth's heart and send feedback readings every thirty minutes. On that tragic morning of September 11, shortly after the first plane hit the first tower in New York, scientists saw the satellite readings shoot right off the charts. What happened to bring such a dramatic effect to both satellite readings that day?

The natural outpouring of feelings from humanity happened, that's what! This wave of heart-based, authentic emotion shared by people all around the world glued to their TV sets that day, experiencing myriad emotions like fear, sadness, rage, and compassion, was so intense that the magnetic field of our collective human heart spiked the readings of the electromagnetic field of our planet.

Braden reminds us that morning of destruction toppled many things, including the scientific assumption that everyone and everything is separate and that the inner experiences of human beings have no effect on the outer experiences—both for individuals and for our planet.

To change anything material requires either an electrical or magnetic change in the field. New research reveals that when people collectively gather to intentionally feel light emotions in their hearts, such as compassion and appreciation, while focusing on heavy situations, their shared focus produces measurable results, such as lowered crime rates in cities or lowered casualty counts in war zones.

As I shared before, the electromagnetic field of the human heart is five thousand times stronger than that of the brain. When we consider five thousand times multiplied several times over in a group sharing a loving intention, that is a whole lot of power for positive change. Especially when the change is shared with all of life, our Earth included.

Closing the Circle of Healing

Knowing your thoughts of kindness and compassion create such powerful and far-reaching effects, I want to honor you for all the transformative work you have been doing throughout our time together in this book. You can be sure that the practices that have activated your Creative Intelligence have had an impactful reach and, without using force, you have shared in ways that have lifted the energy in the field naturally!

You have uplifted more than you will ever know by turning your awareness inwardly, even when you felt most alone; in your heaviest moments. I hope it's clear to you now that you are always loved and supported by Source and an integral member of our interconnected human family!

Completing this final step of your healing requires you to continue to Share and express your true colors and all your newfound wisdom from your Creative Intelligence. Holding back will leave your healing journey incomplete while sharing from your heart, either silently or with words, to support another person struggling in their journey will close your circle of healing naturally.

Enjoy your final Creative Spark for Step 7 as you paint and Share a healing blast of love out for our planet Earth, our shared home. I'll meet you in the next chapter in the quiet of your creative space as you make a very special review for yourself.

Refresh and Review

- As your healing journey here with me comes to an end, you can close the circle of learning by sharing with others so they, in turn, can create healing for themselves.

- Seeing another's beauty and infinite potential regardless of how they are showing up is exactly how Source views each of us. You can't help but have an impact on someone when you choose to see them this way.

- From a state of unconditional love, you naturally Share from the quiet of who you are to create healing support for another. If words are needed, you will feel a Divine impulse from your heart center.

- There is a measurable energetic reciprocity between our planet and our humanity. We have the power to impact the Earth's magnetic field as we collectively gather and intentionally feel light emotions while focusing upon regions with heavy challenges that need to heal.

Creative Spark - Step 7

Share It
Create a Blast of Love for All of Earth

- In the quiet of your creative space, gather your crayons, paints, brushes, a tub of water, and a large piece of paper (or two smaller pieces taped together).

- With one hand on your heart and the other on your paper, breathe deeply and slowly, imagining light-filled energy flowing upward from the center of the Earth through your feet, up through your body, and shooting straight out of your head. See that light continue up through the ceiling as it continues up into the blackness of space until you can see a brilliant white light. Connect with the light of the Creator and say, "Creator of all that is, I command you to create a blast of unconditional love for all of Earth as we cocreate here and now. Show me!"

- Open your eyes and then notice what color you're most attracted to. Use this color to either paint or draw a circle the size of your closed fist in the middle of your paper.

- Next, inside the circle, draw two triangles, overlapping, one on top of the other, with the first one pointing upward and the second one pointing downward to form a six-pointed star within your circle.

- Focus on the Earth's many challenges and feel in for which of her many challenges moves you most. Set the one heartfelt challenge that attracted you into the center of the star with a word, symbol, or image to represent it.

- As you draw and color it in, reflect upon the six steps that you have learned so far: "Own It," "Ask on It," "Receive from It," "Act on It," "Expect it," and "Love it."

- Paint six lines that radiate out from each of the six points of the star. Paint them to the far edge of your paper. While you are painting these six lines, move the challenge you chose on behalf of the planet through each of the steps and upcycle it to receive any insights or intuitive hints of wisdom as you do. Keep open to what messages the Universe has for you.

- Just as last time, begin to paint into this radiant star, keeping your focus on your love for our planet as you do. Step-by-step, point by point, fill your paper with the colors that light you up and express your gratitude for our planet and for all of her inhabitants.

- Take your time and enjoy all the feelings that flow through you as you ply your unique colors into and all around the radiating star. See its beams of love and light blasting out for all to receive from each point.

- Continue painting until you feel complete. Take time to look upon its radiance to receive all the love it's flowing back to you. Take in any messages that our planet shares with you as you create. Remember, when you create healing for another, the energy you give out comes straight back to you.

**Imagine this taking place for you now—
See it, feel it, be it!**

Your Turn Now

"The best way to predict your future is to create it"

—Abraham Lincoln

Chapter 12

Let It Create You: Becoming a Life in Full Colors

Here it is, the last chapter of the book. If you're still here with me now, then I know you are in your creative flow and you have been doing the work!

That's the thing when you learn something new. It takes some effort and can feel like work until you do it enough times that it becomes second nature. Expect that to happen with everything you have learned here in these pages. Soon enough, these seven steps will pop into your awareness at the moment you need them like a Divine notification from your Creative Intelligence.

You will get to the place where you don't even need to go to your physical creative space to pivot heaviness for the light. You have your inner creative space and your imagination joining you wherever you go. Each of the creative processes you learned here, using paper, paint, and colored crayons, can also be done with invisible art materials in your imaginal world as well.

This is how you process your challenges energetically, and it works quickly and effectively too! Whether you move energy with a paintbrush on paper or with the crayons in your imagination is of no difference. Do whatever works for you in the moments that you need to creatively alchemize heavy emotions.

You know full well from experience that each and every trigger, frustration, pain point, and full-blown struggle that shows up is an opportunity to grow and create something new. Keep open and curious about those challenging, heavy-hued visitors. Remember that we all have them drop by. Receive them with curious expectation, as you know how to upcycle them for the light and wisdom they hold.

As you've transformed your challenge here through these pages, you're likely feeling more than alright with the landscape of your life. Even if nothing changed outwardly, your inner world is certainly activated and aligned with your Source, who loves to cocreate with you.

Be easy and patient with yourself and remember that we are all a continual becoming. There are colorful pieces within us that are shifting, changing, and ever in process. This is how we can be easy and patient with those around us as well. Especially with the ones whose colors seems to clash with ours.

We all are struggling with something. Even the shiniest looking ones on social media have heavy-hued challenges in their lives.

Take a moment now and think of where you were when you started this colorful journey here and where you are now as it circles to a close. Honor all that has transpired and transformed in you. Breathe it all into your beautiful heart and let it sink into every cell in your body.

I wonder if you can close your eyes and get a sense of the powerful Creative Intelligence that is pulsing through you, living you, guiding you, carrying you, and loving you unconditionally.

Can you feel that? Can you sense the energy moving through you?

Connect with that Life Force often. Pause and breathe and feel. Rest and relax into it and know that you are never living your moments all by your yourself. Your Creator is with you and cocreating through you to expand the radiant and wonderous expression you are!

Let these seven steps become your own precious power tools for creating transformation for your life. They will never break or lose their strength and they have great effect on all those who use them regularly. Best of all, they are known to cause all areas of your life to run a lot more harmoniously. So, pick 'em up often and don't leave them waiting in the shed.

Your Invitation to Integrate

While it seems that we are coming towards the end of our journey here, if we think about closing circles, then the ending disappears to bring around a whole new beginning. And just like that, a brand-new space is opening up right here and now for you. A space just for you to create, to consolidate, to integrate, and to celebrate all you have learned, lived, and received!

For this to happen well for you, there's only one thing left to do, and that is to hand the creation of this final chapter over to you. It's time, Dear Creator, to flow your colorful Creative Intelligence into these final pages and directly into your life.

As I hand things over to you now, stay close to your heart, which holds the key to every door that appears before you. Remember Joseph Campbell's words here: "Doors will open where you would not have thought there would be doors, and where there wouldn't be a door for anyone else."

Enjoy being the Master Creator of your Life in Full Colors. Welcome all your feelings while honoring and upcycling your heavy ones for the light. As you create, lean into life deeply, notice the wonderous tiny details, and breathe it all in—every color, every hue, and every form that shows up just for you!

Now, tuck yourself into your special creative space and set all your colors out around you. Ensure you won't be disturbed as you let the silence of your inner space support you. Ready? It's your turn now!

Create a Review of Your Healing Journey
Review Your Creative Sparks and Creative Exercises

- Flip through the pages and revisit each creative exercise you did throughout the book. Review both the embedded exercises within the chapters and the Creative Sparks at the ends of the chapters too.

- Set all the artwork you created on paper or in your art journal in front of you. Lay it out in chronological order like a personal gallery for you to feel, experience, and review.

- Take your time as you take in all your artwork again. Revisit your entire healing journey; allow yourself to sense into everything—visually and energetically.

- In your journal or in the space below, write out what you're feeling, what you're noticing, what surprises and delights you, and what patterns and themes are being made visible to you through your artwork for your life.

Revisit Refresh and Review

- Revisit all the learning points set at the close of each chapter within the section called "Refresh and Review."

- In your own way (through symbols, words, images, doodles), notice and record the key points that stand out most that you want to take with you from this journey. Fill the whole page with the colors that attract you.

- Take a picture and set it as the wallpaper on your mobile phone. Look at these key points often, knowing that words have energy and power. Speak them out loud into your mirror as you look into your beautiful eyes, which are the windows to your soul. Let these words guide you going forward.

Review of All That's Transformed within You

- Reflect upon all that you have learned and transformed within yourself in this journey.

- Create a drawing or painting (or a combination mixed media piece) on a piece of paper or in the space that follows if you prefer. It's time to celebrate the Creative Intelligence you are!

- Consider all the transformative changes within and around you that have come about because of all the healing work you have done. Breathe deeply and slowly as you flow out the colors, shapes, and lines that best express your heart right now.

- Relax into this and have fun knowing that as you focus your attention and elevate your emotions while you play this way, you are naturally creating heart coherence, which benefits you and all those around you.

- Let this artwork be your heart's song. Your authentic expression, in any form, is a gift to yourself, your family and friends, and all of humanity. Repeat this exercise often as you upcycle future challenges that come to you for transformation.

Receive All the Love That's Streaming to You

This final review is one I highly recommend you return to routinely after you complete this book. This is the most important practice you could implement on a regular basis to reinforce all the work you've done.

Think back through your lifetime and reflect upon these questions: When was the last time you sat down and wrote a heart-filled, tear-jerker love letter to someone? Have you ever written such a love letter to yourself? Often, we fail to speak loving words to ourselves, let alone write a no-holds-barred love letter.

Now is the chance for you to feel and experience the love of the Universe pouring through your pen and onto the paper in the space that follows. A love letter just for you!

- Close your eyes, put your non-writing hand on your heart, and feel all the love and appreciation for yourself and all that you have created with your colorful life.

- If you don't know how to start, my love letters often begin with "My Dear Darling Corry…" or a variation of this. Let this be a mushy, gushy love letter directly to you from the Source of Life itself. It will likely feel uncomfortable and unnatural the first time you do it. Don't worry; this is normal. Don't let it stop you, however. Keep on and write through any uncomfortable feelings

- Begin in your heart, as always, slowing your breath and focusing on love and gratitude.

- Let your writing hand flow a page or two (or even more) of pure unconditional love to you. Feel every word streaming directly into you as you write! Keep some tissues nearby; it's very moving to receive pure Divine love in this form.

- Once you feel complete, take it all in, read it out loud, and feel the love enter each and every piece of you again. You can never have too much love. Keep this letter somewhere safe and remember to read it often to remind you the truth of Source's love for you.

Corry MacDonald

Just Before You Lift Off

By now, dear Creative One, after all the love and care you created for yourself through your journey here, you are likely feeling lighter than ever and ready to fly from these pages into your colorful life. Before you lift off, though, I want to pause and offer a heartfelt thank you.

Thank you for following your inner impulse to tuck into this book here with me. Thank you for trusting yourself and looking inwardly. Thank you for upcycling your heaviness into light so wonderfully. Thank you for Creating Healing for yourself and for all of us in the web of life, as we all benefit energetically.

You are a precious gift and a natural healer. By honoring your innate Creative Intelligence, all your true colors naturally express through you and into the world.

Walk tall and in your joy as you create your radiant life. Step forward fearlessly into every opportunity-filled challenge, knowing you are never walking alone. You are being lived by a Force of Love that is supporting you and always present to cocreate with

Corry MacDonald

you. This same Universal Love brought us together, here within these pages, to discover what we all came for—a Life in Full Colors!

Big Love,
X Corry

"If ever there was a time that Life needed you to move through each moment as the colorful radiant Creative Intelligence that you are, it is now!"

—Corry MacDonald

Ready to Create More?

If you want to continue your learning, visit "The Courses" at www.creatinghealingwithcorry.com.

In her online course series, which is taught in three phases consecutively, Corry deepens the teachings in *Life in Full Colors*.

Additional services to access through the website to lighten your colorful journey include:

- Free resources
- A free guided meditation
- Digital downloads of Corry's artwork
- Public speaking for events, summits, and podcasts
- Bespoke Creating Healing workshops for groups, either in person or online
- Private healing sessions with Corry, either in person or online

Manufactured by Amazon.ca
Bolton, ON

17811492R00133